CANDLE
BURNING
RITUALS

CANDLE BURNING RITUALS

marie bruce

quantum

LONDON • NEW YORK • TORONTO • SYDNEY

quantum

An imprint of W. Foulsham & Co. Ltd
The Publishing House, Bennetts Close,
Cippenham, Slough, Berkshire, SL1 5AP, England

ISBN 0–572–02692-7

Printed in Great Britain by St. Edmundsbury Press, Bury St. Edmunds, Suffolk.

Contents

Introduction

For the majority of people in today's world, the word magic conjures up images of darkly robed old women bending over simmering cauldrons, chanting incantations and summoning spirits. Yet true magic is a completely natural practice and practitioners of magic use various techniques on a regular basis to influence and improve their lives.

Anyone can learn to work magic with surprisingly positive results. You do not need to be a witch to cast a spell and achieve the result you want, nor do you need to be a student of the Craft or the occult in general. With the right intentions, plenty of directed focus and a good instruction manual, you can learn how to cast spells that get positive results, and you can empower yourself for a better life.

One of the most popular forms of magic is that of candle magic. Candleburning rituals have been used for centuries, and continue to be used in the new millennium by people from all walks of life. Perhaps the popularity of candle magic is largely due to its simplicity – anyone can light a candle! Add to this simplicity the effectiveness of a candleburning ritual and you are definitely on to a winner.

As a working witch I use this form of magic on an almost daily basis. Whatever the problem, whatever the need or request, there is a candleburning ritual to match. For me, candles are one of the most enjoyable aspects of the Craft, and one of my most useful tools. The warm, comforting light that candles give cannot fail to charm, and will also help you to relax and release the stresses of the day in a non-intrusive way. Candles can be used to brighten our lives and can turn our homes into magical areas full of little sparks of light.

Within the pages of this book are candleburning rituals for virtually every purpose, with tips on how to adapt any ritual to suit your own particular needs. We will also look at creating a candleburning altar, advanced candle spells and step-by-step rituals of passion, prosperity, protection and power, as well as techniques for incorporating fragrant herbs, oils and incenses into your candle magic to increase the power of your spell castings.

In this grimoire, or spell book, of candle magic, you are sure to find a spell to suit you. May the flame of magic burn bright within your life.

Blessed be

Morgana (Marie Bruce)

Warning

Always take care when using candles. Ensure that they are secured safely in a candle holder or similar, do not stand them too close to curtains or other hanging fabric, and never leave them unattended.

Care should also be taken when using essential oils, as they can cause irritation if applied directly to the skin. Follow the instructions on page 63 with regard to using carrier oils. If you are pregnant or breast-feeding, seek medical advice about which oils are safe to use. Synthetic oils are best avoided since they are not all suitable for use in candle rituals (see pages 56–7).

CHAPTER 1

Understanding magic

Before you can work a candle spell effectively, it is vital that you have a sound knowledge of magic in general. That is not to say that you must have practised magic for the last ten years, but you must read through these chapters carefully and absorb their teachings. Here you will find everything you need to know to begin practising successful candleburning rituals.

Also, I strongly recommend that you read through this book from beginning to end before trying out any of the spells. In this way, you will have a secure foundation of magical knowledge and any spells you subsequently cast will therefore be much stronger and more powerful.

The purpose of this book is to teach anyone who reads it, whatever their background and magical experience, to become a powerful and successful worker of candle magic. This power will mean that you can take any aspect of your life and significantly improve it with magic. True magic is so much more than spells and potions. It is connecting the power of the human mind with the unlimited power of universal energies, using spells and magical tools as a focus.

Witches are not the only ones capable of casting spells, although most witches, myself included, do work magic on a regular basis. The word witch comes from the old English word 'wyk', which means 'to bend and shape'. This is precisely what witches do: we bend and shape our lives to our own liking using magic and spells. But magic is available to everyone, of every age, race and background. Magic is universal because it uses universal energies. Many books on candle magic are aimed specifically at the witch and others on the New Age path. (True witchcraft is actually a spiritual belief and not all workers of magic are witches.) This book is written for all people of all religions, and as such does not refer to any particular deity. Instead I refer simply to the higher powers or spirit, leaving you free to incorporate your own personal religion and deity name into your candleburning rituals.

If you do not follow any spiritual path, simply focus on your inner power – many of the spells are constructed in this way, and it can often bring about the best results.

Magic is a very personal thing, and as you become more experienced you will become fully aware of your power. Magic is not a force outside of yourself, it dwells deep within, waiting for you to bring it out. You are the magic. The magic is you. And of course, when performed correctly, spells are very effective. If candle rituals didn't work, I wouldn't be writing this book, which is itself the result of a candle spell! Spell casting continues to work for me, and it can work for anyone who remains focused on their magical goal.

But what exactly is magic? We have already mentioned the phrase 'to bend and shape', but magic is more than that. It is a series of actions, used in conjunction with a focused mind, in order to will positive change into manifestation. Magic is more than a wish list or a feeble hope. It is a belief, a conviction that your spell will work and the change will occur.

The practitioner's will

As soon as you begin to work magic and cast spells, you are a magical person. From the moment you picked up this book, you stepped on to the path that means you have taken full control of your life.

Generally, people fall into two categories: passive and active. Passive people constantly worry and complain, even when things are going well. They often feel that the tide of life is sweeping them along and they are powerless to stop it. The majority of the world is made up of passive people and, if we are honest, this stereotype has taken possession of all of us at some point in our lives. This is no bad thing, for it gives us an opportunity to step back from life and reflect on where we are heading. The danger lies in being constantly passive, as this will get you nowhere, and will mean that your dreams remain just that.

Active people are always excited about something. They see life as a wonderful and precious experience and they are determined to live it to the full. They are determined to succeed, whatever the odds. They aim for the moon and know that the only one to get them there is themselves.

Which of these stereotypes do you think is the more powerful? The second one, of course. Active people are in control of their lives. They don't wait for life's ambitions to be handed to them, instead they use their energies and will power to manifest their dreams. They are the magical people.

Will power and the power of the mind are the first and foremost tools of magic. No spell can be cast effectively without will power. No positive change can occur without the power of the mind. We are what we think, therefore to work rituals and be magical, we must think magically.

Although this may sound a little complicated to the beginner, it is something that every human being does on a daily basis without even being aware of it. Our minds are complex computers and we are the ones who program them. Therefore we create our own lives. For example, if you see a beautiful necklace in a shop window that you would like to buy for yourself or a loved one, and you know you do not have enough money to buy it, you might say to yourself, 'I can't afford it'. In this way you programme both your mind and the universal energies around you into a state of poverty. Thus you will never buy the necklace. This is how the mind, the universe and personal power work. They give you exactly what you ask for. So if you are constantly affirming your lack of money or ill health – you will always be poor and poorly! Because we design our own lives.

Now let's take the same scenario and see how a magical person would deal with it. On looking in her purse a young woman discovers she doesn't have enough money for the beautiful necklace in the shop window. She says to herself, 'I choose not to buy this today. I will come back and purchase it another day.' Thus she has already stated her intention of purchasing the necklace at a later date. On her return home, she brings the vision of herself wearing the necklace to mind and performs a simple candle spell, all the while focusing on her intent. She lights a candle and says:

I choose to own this necklace. It is coming to me. So be it.

As the candle burns, her intention is taken out into the universe and the magic is in progress. Perhaps she will receive an unexpected sum of money that will enable her to buy the necklace, or maybe someone will buy her the necklace as a gift. However the magic works, the outcome is the same – the spell is effective. It works due to the focused intention of the spell caster's will. Know that you too have this incredible force inside you. You should use the power of your mind and your magical will constantly and positively to reaffirm your magical goal and your life's dreams.

How magic works

Most people hold the belief that magic is a supernatural power. Unfortunately many films, television programmes and works of fiction have added to this belief with their depictions of witches calling up ghosts and summoning demons. Not that there is anything wrong with these forms of entertainment (personally I adore Gothic novels and movies), but the point to be remembered is that they are indeed fictional and have no real bearing on true magic. Real magic – the kind that you are going to perform – is entirely natural and it works in conjunction with the universal laws of nature.

Your power will bring you exactly what you focus on the most, and although all energy has periods of ebb and flow, generally, if your intent and need are strong enough, you can manifest your greatest desires into your life. Magic does not go against the laws of nature, it works with them. The world is a naturally abundant place and is naturally balanced. Human laws and human behaviour have created the concepts of poverty, lack and unbalance. Poverty is a man-made problem spawned from human greed – abundance and enough for all is the natural order of things. Magical spells work within the laws of nature and will thus enable you to regain balance in your life, and to be in harmony with nature and the universal energies.

Magic always travels the path of least resistance. This means that if you cast a spell for £100, the money will manifest into your life in a normal, routine way such as a tax return, money paid back to you from an over-charged utility bill, or overtime to the value of your spell. Of course, you might win the money on the lottery and this would certainly 'feel' more magical, but if the money arrives from a mundane source – then just be thankful and accept the overtime!

All too often, newcomers to magic cast a spell and expect nothing short of a miracle. Magic does work, but in the most unexpected and often understated ways. On many occasions, your spell may manifest but you will fail to recognise it. This is especially likely to happen in the beginning when you are new to magic.

Magical rule number one: There's no such thing as coincidence.

Everything that happens has a reason. When your spells manifest into your life, even in the most mundane ways, don't put it down to coincidence. Acknowledge your power and recognise the fact that your spell worked. You made it happen, with your will power, with your mind – with your magic!

Although spells are fun to perform, they should be taken seriously, and you must personally do everything you can to ensure the success of the spell, which leads us to the next rule.

Magical rule number two: Always back up your spells in the mundane world.

All the job spells in the world aren't going to get you your ideal employment unless you fill out application forms and attend interviews. If you cast a spell for a new love interest, your ideal partner is unlikely to come walking into your front room. You need to get out and meet people as a way of backing up your spell.

Every spell you cast, every candle ritual you perform, should be backed up with action in the mundane world. The universal energies will not assist your power unless you are willing to help yourself. This is part of being a magical person and a spell caster. You must take full control of your life and change anything you don't like about it with spells *and* mundane action.

Does this mean that spells aren't powerful? Absolutely not. By working spells your subsequent action in the mundane world will be so much easier because it has magic attached to it. Many overweight people would like to be slim, and there are candle rituals to effect this change – but only if the practitioner eats sensibly and exercises more. These spells will not work in conjunction with a diet of king-size chocolate bars, chips and pizza! However, the spell will assist with hunger pangs and cravings, and will add magic to any exercise plan, thus making the goal that much easier to achieve. The practitioner may wonder at a sudden passion for step class! As a serious practitioner of magic, you must remember to reinforce all your spell workings by taking action. Even one small step takes you that much nearer to your goal.

Magical ethics

Because spells are so powerful, there are certain rules that should be abided by. With so much energy flying around, from both yourself and the universe, it is essential that you take care and direct your focus properly.

The 'harm none' rule: If it harms none (including yourself), then do what you will with your magic. Never use this power to hurt any other living creature, or to control anyone other than yourself.

The rule of three: Ever mind the rule of three – what you send out comes back to thee.

These rules are taken from the witches' religion of Wicca, but they can be found in any religion the world over. The words used may be different but the message is the same. If you ignore these rules, then your negative action will rebound on you with three times the force and three times the consequences. Positive spells will also come back to you with three times the force, bringing more positivity into your life. Many people know this as the concept of karma. Keep your karma slate clean and you won't go far wrong.

Choice, not chance

As a worker of magic you have now taken control of your life. This also means that you have taken complete and full responsibility for everything you say, do and even think. Life is a game of choice, not chance. We may not always like the particular choices life puts to us, but we always have a choice. We make choices every day of our lives – some good, some bad – but in the end the choice is always ours to make.

For instance, you chose to pick up this book. You chose to read it. Now you can either choose to put it in a drawer and forget about it, or you can choose to use its teachings and so improve your life significantly. It is all about choice.

When working rituals you will be faced with many choices. What tools to use, when to perform the spell, what words to say, which goal to aim for first. By absorbing the information in this book however, you will be equipped to make an informed choice, and that is the key to effective magic and life transformation. You must always make an informed choice. If you do not have the information you need, then ask for it, or search for it on your own, but never make a magical choice without first having the information to hand.

The magical need

All spells should be born of a need. In fact this is the best way to ensure success. If you truly need what you ask for, your power will bring it to you.

If you find yourself short of cash with no food in the cupboards and three hungry children to feed, then by performing a needy spell you will make sure that you receive help from some earthly source. This could be in the form of a new job, an unexpected windfall, or even a state benefit you didn't know you were entitled to. I have cast many a money spell and I have never been left without some form of financial assistance. Personally, this tends to come in the form of a writing commission, but money spells can be answered in many different ways.

If you need money don't be afraid to 'spell' for it (a witchy term – we 'spell' for what we want), but make sure your need is genuine. If you would like to be wealthy magic can help, but you must word your spell carefully. By casting for an opportunity to improve your current financial status, you are accepting responsibility. However much you may love to dream about it, having a huge amount of money may not be good for you. If you couldn't handle being a millionaire, your spell won't work. Spells cast out of pure greed are usually doomed to failure. Always be realistic in your spell-casting goals; don't waste your time casting spells that you know in your heart won't work.

In order for your spells to have the best possible chance of manifestation, they must be backed up by a genuine need, but this need doesn't have to be great, nor should you wait until you are in a state of absolute desperation. If you need the baby to stop crying so that you can have a much-needed nap, light a candle and focus on your intent. In all likelihood you and baby will peacefully nod off together!

Be careful what you wish for ...

Never have these words been more true than with magic. Before you perform any type of candle spell, you must be absolutely certain that you can handle the outcome. Magic does work, so it should never be performed in a state of anger or revenge. Always think through the possible outcomes of your spell, and not just the obvious ones either. What could be the most outlandish and unexpected way for your spell to manifest? Could you deal with this form of manifestation? Magic has a way of taking you by surprise. Many a witch has cast a spell for a companion in life and been given a puppy or a cat. By failing to state that they wanted a human companion, they left their spells open to interpretation. Thus the power obliged in the most straightforward way. Remember, magic takes the path of least resistance.

You must always word your spell very carefully. Let's say that you are unhappy in your current employment and you cast a spell so that you 'never have to see the place again'. The path of least resistance could be redundancy, dismissal or even a long-term illness that prevents you from going into work. Because your spell stated no alternative form of employment, only a desire to remove

yourself from your present employment, the probable outcome of the spell is – no more employment. Be careful what you wish for – you just might get it! A spell to get you out of an unhappy source of employment should always contain the wish for happier, better or equally paid employment. Without this you could find yourself in a very sticky spot.

Clarity is the key to magic. Think through your reasons for casting a spell, think through the basic intention of the spell, and lastly, think through all the possible ways your spell could be effective. Word your spells with extreme care. If necessary write them out two or three times, then at the end of every single spell you work, add the words:

I cast this spell with harm to none.

This will ensure that your spell has only a positive outcome for anyone involved.

All this emphasises that magic should not be taken casually but, on the contrary, that you should be thoughtful and considerate in all your magic and think each spell through carefully before you cast it.

Note that revenge should never be the intention of any of your spells. Leave this to karma, which will do a far better job than you could anyway.

Always cast your own spells

It is very important that you cast your own spells. Do not leave this important power in the hands of anyone else, however much you love and trust them. This is for one very simple reason – you are the creator of your own life, you are the source of your own power. Therefore, no one can cast a spell for you as powerfully and effectively as you can cast it for yourself. Because you are the main participant in your life, it stands to reason that you should also be the main participant in your magic. You are the power. You are the magic. Never hand the magical reins over to someone else. They may not take you in the direction you want to go. Keep hold of your power and be the master of your own magic.

The flip side of this is that you should not work magic for others without their permission. This includes all positive magic and healing rituals. It is always better to show them how to work magic for themselves. Remember the proverb:

> *Give a man a fish and you feed him for a day.*
> *Give him the means to fish and he feeds himself for a lifetime.*

So it is with spells and rituals. If people come to you for help magically, it is far better to give them the means rather than the result. Of course you should support them and share your knowledge, but show them the path so that they can find their own way, their own power, their own magic.

Finally, never work magic out of desperation. Cast spells regularly on the basis that 'prevention is better than cure'. A desperate person is an out-of-control, powerless person.

When spells don't work

Everyone has set-backs, as I'm sure did Merlin and the witches of old. So if your spell doesn't work, don't worry about it. Go through the spell and look for any cracks or possible weaknesses. Was your timing correct? Were your words spoken with authority and with clarity?

If everything in your spell seems fine, cast it again. Wait at least one lunar month for manifestation, longer for big spells. If your spell still hasn't worked, it generally means that what you are casting for is not right for you at this time. Magic will only work if it is to improve our lives and be for our highest good. Don't give up. Move on to another, perhaps smaller goal and work on that. Everything, including magic, takes practice. Don't worry if things go wrong or don't turn out as you expected them to. It usually means that something even bigger and better is on the way.

The code of successful spell casting

You may have thought that it was only chivalrous knights of old who lived by a code of honourable conduct. In fact, there is much to be learned from the knights of the old code that could perhaps bring a sense of peace and security to our modern, crime-ridden world.

As a worker of magic it is important that you adhere to a code of conduct. I have therefore devised the following code of honour as a guideline to help you get the most from your rituals:

1   Always follow the 'harm none' rule.

2   Always observe the rule of three.

3   Reinforce all spells in the mundane world.

4   Always make an informed choice.

5   Perform only magic that is born of a need.

6   Perform all magic with strength, honour and clarity.

7   Always be the master of your own magic.

8   Never cast spells on other people.

9   Be supportive and guiding to seekers on the magical path.

10 Cast spells to improve and retain control of your own life.

CHAPTER 2
Elements of magic

Our entire universe is made up of four elements: water, earth, air and fire. In a magical sense these elements are both physical and ethereal, residing on both the physical and astral planes at one and the same time. It is for this reason that the elements are used in spells. By taking a physical representation of the element, we can connect with its astral twin and so create magic.

Much of element magic is symbolic, and each element has its own area of magical use. In candle rituals, the most obvious element present is that of fire, yet the three remaining elements are also in full magical use. It is important that you study each element in depth so that you are aware of which powers you are using and how their energies differ. True candle magic is more than a candle and a match. It is bringing together various energies and directing them towards your need. The candle then becomes a physical representation of that need.

For magic to work at its best, all four elements should be represented in some way. In candle rituals the candle itself represents earth, the flame is obviously fire, the smoke represents air and the melted wax is symbolic of water. For all the elements to be represented in a single magical tool is rare, yet this does illustrate why candleburning rituals are so powerfully effective.

Just as the candle represents the elements, the elements in turn represent various magical goals and areas of life. For example, should you wish to cast a love spell, you would use the element of fire, as fire is associated with love and passion.

To assist magically with mending a broken leg, you would use water, as this is the element associated with healing. You would, of course, go to hospital and get the leg set first. Magic should be used in conjunction with, not instead of, medical attention.

All the elements have a corresponding colour, season, magical hour (dawn, noon, dusk or midnight) and direction. These directions can be found either by using a compass or, alternatively, by labelling the point opposite you as you enter your magical area or look at your altar as twelve o'clock – the other points can then be found using a clock face. The elements also have particular powers, so let's examine them a little more carefully.

Water

I have to admit that water is my favourite element, particularly in the form of an ocean. The powers of water are quite gentle and they help us to achieve balance, harmony, inner peace and tranquillity. The water element can also assist in matters of stress, dreams, health, psychic powers and gentle cleansings.

The colour of water is blue, the direction west, the magical hour dusk and the season autumn. Therefore a blue candle placed at nine o'clock is ideal. A bowl of water with floating candles would also be appropriate. Water is a receptive energy and its tides can pull positive things towards you and negative things away from you. To attune with this element, go to the beach, paddle in a stream, have a long soak in a hot bath or place a water feature in your home or garden. The bathroom is associated with water and is an excellent place to perform self-healing. Rubbing oils on to candles incorporates this element into your rituals.

Earth

The earth is our home and as such we have a very special connection with this particular element. The powers of earth can be used for all spells of fertility, stability and growth. Earth also rules over finances, the home, career, savings and prosperity.

The colour of earth is green, and its direction north, so you would place a green candle at twelve o'clock. The season of earth is winter, when mother earth takes her much needed rest, and the magical hour is midnight. Earth energy is receptive, which means that it is a good element for pulling things towards you. You can attune with this element in parks, gardens, caves, mines and forests. In the home, the kitchen is the earth room. To incorporate this element into your rituals, use herbs and bury the candle stub in the garden. Thus the candle ritual also becomes an earth spell.

Air

Without air our entire world and all in it would die. It is the element most vital to our survival. Magically the powers of air are used in spells for creativity, inspiration, intelligence, tests and examinations, vocal and musical talents and the arts.

The colour of air is yellow, its direction east, dawn is the magical hour and the season is spring, so a yellow candle placed at three o'clock would be appropriate. As air is a projective energy it can be used in two ways: to remove negative aspects from your life, and to project yourself or your efforts forward in the world. Musicians, poets, singers and dancers often feel an affinity with this element – they are unconsciously invoking its powers.

To attune with air, feel the wind in your hair, climb a hill or a mountain, observe the clouds, collect fallen feathers and listen to music, particularly wind instruments. In the home, the most creative room in the house is associated with air. This could be the living room, study, library or home office. If you would like to incorporate the element of air into your candleburning rituals, then burn incense and wrap the candle stub in cotton wool once it has finished burning.

Fire

This is the most obvious element of candle magic. Fire can be warmth and comfort, or death and destruction, so you must be very careful how you use this particular element. In magic, fire spells are cast for love, passion, transformation, protection, strength, courage and to cleanse.

The colour of fire is obviously red. Its direction is south, its magical hour is noon, and its season is the heat of summer. By placing a red candle at six o'clock you are invoking the powers of this element. Again, fire is a projective energy and you can use it symbolically to burn things – with harm to none, of course.

Attuning with fire is as simple as sunbathing, lighting a candle, watching the flames of an open fire or enjoying a good summer barbecue. In the home, the bedroom is the area of passion and thus of fire.

Fire magic

Although candles are the most popular form of fire magic, they are by no means the only form. Fire magic can be performed using many tools such as a barbecue, a bonfire, an indoor fireplace, a gas stove or oven, a gas fire – even an electric light bulb or torch. Fire magic can also be performed using the greatest fire of all, the sun, not to mention such things as matches, lighters, fireworks and sparklers. Candles are just one option open to you, and as you become more experienced in your magic you may like to experiment a little, always bearing in mind, of course, that fire magic must always go hand in hand with a regard for safety.

CHAPTER 3

Preparing for ritual

So far we have looked at the ethics of magic and the power of the elements in magic. In this chapter we will look at the components of spell casting. Although candleburning rituals are simple to perform, you will give yourself a better chance of success if you first learn the basics of magical technique. When you can perform magic under any circumstances, you will be truly competent and on your way to becoming what is termed as an 'adept'. Working magic is more than an unusual pastime. It is a power that carries with it much responsibility.

As with any new skill, there will invariably be some aspects of magic that you find easier than others. This is natural and it is important that you know your own limitations from the beginning. Only then will you be in a position to reinforce your strengths whilst at the same time working on your weaknesses. Magic itself has no limits and is completely boundless. It is only our own limitations that restrict our spell casting. Becoming magically adept takes hard work and commitment on your part; you will not reach a level of competence overnight. The ability to cast spells will, however, increase your power over your own life and will gradually alter your life for the better.

You will probably find yourself looking forward to the time you spend casting spells, and will scour the bookstores for volumes on magic in order to increase your knowledge. With your first successful spell comes a profound hunger for increased ability, which will only be fed by studying and practising a wealth of magical techniques. When it comes to magic, you will find that the more you know, the more you want to know. As with life, we are forever learning, no matter how experienced we may or may not be. There's always more to discover.

Sympathetic magic

Magic works on the principle that like attracts like. This concept is known as sympathetic magic: what you focus on the most is what your power will bring to you. For instance, if you focus on your lack of money, your power will be tuned into the concept of poverty and so that is what you will get. By the same token then, if you focus on gaining money, your power will bring you abundance.

Candleburning rituals are one of the oldest forms of sympathetic magic. The colour, inscription and shape of the candle are chosen very carefully and are used to represent in a physical way the required magical goal. The candle becomes a trigger for the spell caster's focus and an expression on the material plane of the spell caster's will.

Candle spells also prove that magic does not have to be complicated to be effective.

Universal waves

Just as the oceans of the earth have a tidal pattern of ebb and flow, so too do the energy waves of the universe. It is these energy waves that bring the manifestation of your spell. All universal energies, whatever their natural form, follow this same tidal pattern and can be identified in our daily lives as periods of action and periods of rest.

In order to use these energy tides in your magic, you must learn their pattern by observing your life carefully and continuously. In general, when the tide of your life is in, there will be a period of many events, either good or bad, that are brought to you on these universal waves of energy. When the tide of life is out, however, you will notice that you experience a period of quiet. This may be positively resting, or negatively stagnating, depending largely on your current mental focus.

To use these tidal energies in your magic, you must always be vigilant in your positive focus. Take note of when your personal tide comes in (you may find it helps to keep a personal diary that you can refer back to). At this point, focus hard on what you most desire – your most sought-after goal. As the tide then moves out, you can either enjoy the period of rest, or use this pull of energy to take away a bad habit, excess weight or any other negative aspect of your life you wish to be free of.

Take a moment right now and think back over the past six months of your life. What events have taken place during this time? Are these events positive or negative in nature? Do you need to alter your mental focus in any way? Which period of tidal flow is your life in right now? How can you use these natural energies to gain the fullest advantage from them and take you closer to your life's goal? By answering these questions and observing your life continuously you will be in a very strong magical position. You will be able to use the universal energies as you will, rather than have your life dictated to you by events seemingly out of your control. Your life is your own, and it is up to you to make your life into something truly magical. Observing and using these energy waves will help you to do just that.

The moon

Both the universal tides of energy and the tides of the oceans are governed by the dominant body of the moon. It is a scientific fact that the moon has a magnetic pull on the ebb and flow of the earth's tides. The moon is also deemed to have influence over the menstrual cycle of women. The magical person cannot afford to overlook such power, and the cycle of the moon is of significant importance when working spells and rituals. To time your spell correctly, you must be able to recognise which phase the moon is in. The easiest way to do this is to look in your diary for the date of the full moon, then observe the phases until you become familiar with them. All the spells in this book give a suggested lunar phase and it is advisable that you work your candleburning rituals at the recommended time to achieve the best results.

Magic should be performed when you have an emotional attachment to the specified outcome of the spell. When your positive feelings run strongest, you are at your most powerful. By aligning these feelings with the correct moon phase, you are giving yourself the best possible chance of success. When planning a spell casting, your first consideration should be the moon phase, and whether or not, in its current position, it is conducive to your magical goal. However, if you are in real need and your spell is an emergency, then cast it anyway, whatever the phase of the moon.

The specific movements of the moon are a complicated science, but for the purposes of magic you need only understand a few basic phases of the moon's cycle, and they are as follows:

New moon: When the moon first appears in the sky as a thin sliver of light.

Waxing moon: When the moon grows each night from new to full.

Full moon: When the moon is seen as a perfect disc of light.

Waning moon: When the moon shrinks in size each night.

Dark moon: When no moon is visible in the sky.

Blue moon: When two full moons appear within the same calendar month.

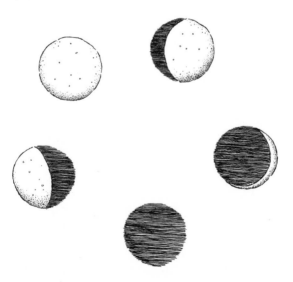

For the purposes of magic, each moon phase has its own particular uses. Magic worked at the new moon should be for new beginnings, new ventures, new life and new opportunities. The new moon is also associated with innocence and childhood so any spells concerning pregnancy or children could be effectively cast at this time.

The waxing moon is growing stronger by the night, so all spells of increase or gain should be worked under this moon. Magic that works to bring something into your life, such as a job or money owed to you, is also within the province of the waxing moon.

The most powerful phase of the moon is when it is full and this phase is good for all types of magic. When in doubt as to the correct moon phase for any particular spell, simply use the full moon. Both the night before and the night after the full moon can be used as part of this phase, giving you three working nights of full moon energy.

The power of the waning moon should be used to remove things from your life. This includes spells cast to lose weight, get out of debt, stop smoking and so on. The magnetic pull of this lunar phase will help carry away any negative aspects of your life in as natural and painless a way as possible.

The dark moon is generally a period of rest and only two types of magic are worked during this phase: bindings (drawing something to you) and banishings (driving something from you).

The blue moon is known in magic as the goal-setting moon and you should never waste this powerful time in the lunar cycle. Always perform at least one goal-setting technique (see page 137) and one goal-getting ritual. Often the smaller goals will manifest by the next full moon, thus giving you an indication that your magic is working and that the larger goals are on their way to you.

Timing

One of the first question beginners ask is: 'How long will it take a spell to work?' The answer is that it depends entirely on the type of spell and magical goal. Although magic is never instantaneous, smaller goals will manifest more quickly than large goals. Magic will always work in its own way, in its own time. You cannot rush your power, but this does not mean that you will be left waiting indefinitely. If the need is there, magic will manifest your desire.

Generally speaking, a large goal (such as a new house, for example) will take anything from six months onwards to manifest. To assist the laws of nature in this manifestation, work the same spell for the same goal every full moon until you receive what you spelled for. A smaller goal (like a spell for increased income) will usually take effect before the next full moon, whereas a spell for a dry washing day could seem to be almost instantaneous. As larger goals take longer, the sooner you begin working on them the better.

Magical hours

Another way to enhance your candleburning rituals is to perform them at one of the magical hours: dawn, noon, dusk and, of course, the witching hour – midnight. Of all these times midnight is the strongest, as the veil between the world of the unseen – the world of magic – and our own world, is at its thinnest. Dawn is for spells of new beginning, noon is for completion, and dusk for closure. Many books go into great depth about planetary hours, but this can often be confusing for the beginner. To create positive magic, work in alignment with the moon, and to give your spells an added boost, work at one of the magical hours. At this stage that is all you need do to begin manifesting change in your life.

Lastly, don't get too hung up on when to work magic and when not to. If you are in the mood for spell casting, if you have a need, then by all means get out the candles and make a start. The magical hours and moon phases are there as a guideline and you can always reword your spell so that it is conducive to the moon. For instance, if it is the time of the waning moon you might still want to cast a spell to improve your finances. You know that the waning moon acts to pull things away from you, and so you cast a spell to remove your personal poverty. As the moon waxes again, you would cast the spell you originally thought of. That is the beauty of magic – it can be adapted to suit any situation.

CHAPTER 4

Sacred space

We all have visions of the perfect place to work magic. Mine would be a Gothic castle, on a wind-swept cliff-side overlooking the sea, complete with a bat-infested bell tower at one end, and a turret and balcony at the other! In reality, much of my spell work is performed at the dressing table in my bedroom, or at the mantlepiece above the fireplace, both of which I have converted into magical altars. A long way from my dream, but such is life – for the moment anyway. The future is mine to create!

The truth is that if we wait for our perfect environment we will never perform magic. Making successful magic is like living in years of hardship – you have to learn to 'make do and mend'. With experience you will be able to manifest your ideal environment but, depending on how elaborate your dream is, this can take time.

Witches and magicians rarely live in cottages at the edge of a dark forest or in baronial manors with secret chambers and underground passages. Instead they live in suburban semis, high-rise flats, inner-city terraced houses, caravans and maisonettes. But wherever we live, our homes are filled with magic, because our lives are filled with magic. I live on the edge of one of the largest cities in England. Every day I see evidence of street vandalism, drug abuse and car crime. Yet my home is a completely safe haven, exuding positive energies because it is a pretty, magical place – and I have made it so.

Creating a magical area in your magical place

Your home is your magical place. It is your own personal area on this vast expanse of land we call the earth. It is also where you will be setting up sacred space, so it is a physical connection with your magic. Whatever your present living arrangements you will need to set aside an area in which to work your candleburning rituals. This is the area within the home where you will keep all your magical tools and where you will create the sacred space of a magical circle when you cast spells.

I am lucky in that I live alone, but you may need to take into consideration the needs of a spouse or the demands of children, not to mention their safety, when you are burning candles. If you have boisterous pets you may need to set up your magical area in a separate room, away from your animal friends. Cats however, tend to enjoy magic and will watch it for hours. I have a big black cat called Pyewackett, who likes nothing better than to sit in the circle with me, mesmerised by the flame of a candle and looking every inch the witch's familiar. However, if your own feline is a mischievous scamp then he is also a fire hazard – it would be better to put him out while you cast your candle spells, in order to avoid accidents.

Make sure your magical area is private. This may mean closing the curtains, locking the door – especially if you share your home with family or friends – and taking the phone off the hook. You might also have to express to other members of your household your wish to be left undisturbed.

Your magical area can be a whole room, or a corner of a room. It could also be a closet, alcove or pantry. You could even make the garden shed into your magical area. If your family or room mates are not sympathetic to your magical tastes, then you can put the items in your magical area into a locked drawer after use for safe keeping. If you have no reason to hide your magical interest then go for it and paint the room silver with gold stars – just kidding! As you become more involved in magic you will want regular access to a place where you can set out your things, cast spells and meditate. The more magic becomes a part of your life, the less you will want to lock your interest away in a cupboard or drawer. A temporary space works as effectively as a permanent one, providing you set it up as often as your circumstances allow, but if you can manage a permanent area, however small, then do make the most of this opportunity.

It is a good idea to have some kind of stereo system set up in your magical area. This should be positioned so that you can reach it while you are in the magical circle. The sound system doesn't have to be top of the range, a basic tape recorder will do. You will then be able to play New Age music and meditational and inspirational tapes. Self-help or positive-thinking tapes are also excellent tools for the magical person. After all, if we are going to change the world, we need to begin with ourselves.

As you work your rituals you will need to think carefully about the type of lighting you have available. Candles are obviously going to be used, but if you are a nervous person you might also like a small lamp to chase away the shadows. A desk lamp might also be useful for when you are making wax talismans and writing spell papers. If you like the dark then just use candles. This, I feel, creates the most magical atmosphere. Overhead lights should be switched off, unless you really cannot manage without them.

Open a window to allow the element of air to circulate and cleanse the whole area. Put up posters and pictures that speak to you of magic, and perhaps add a few fluorescent stars. Bring life into your magical area with potted plants, fresh flowers or maybe some goldfish which, according to the masters of feng shui, attract prosperity into your life.

Try to make your magical area reflect your personal interest in magic. Everyone has items that are special to them, such as diaries, trophies or certificates. Collect these treasures and arrange them carefully, perhaps on a shelf or a windowsill. To proclaim your move to a magical life, go out on a shopping trip and buy something beautiful for your magical area. It could be an oil burner, a carved wooden box to keep your spell candles in, a picture or wall hanging, tasselled velvet cushions to sit on, or a figurine of a wizard or witch.

If finances are a problem, then fear not. Light a candle and ask that nature provide something beautiful that will enhance your magical place. Go out for a walk and keep your eyes peeled. Earlier this summer, my best friend and I were out walking and we found two lovely fallen twigs. Mine is shaped like a pair of stag antlers and hers looks just like a sword. We both use these gifts of nature in our rituals. Magical tools don't have to be expensive to be beautiful – and sometimes they are free. Be aware of what is around you, keep your magical eyes open and you'll be amazed at what you find.

Two things that you might wish to have in your area of magic are a bookcase for your magical texts and a cupboard or chest for all your magical tools. This will save time, and things are less likely to get lost! Once you have made your chosen area magical, you are then ready to create sacred space.

What is sacred space?

The area within a magical circle is called sacred space, and is totally free of all negativity. This is where you should work your magical spells.

Personally I regard my entire house as sacred space because I regularly cast a magical circle around the whole of my property. However, I still cast a magical circle around myself and my altar when I am about to perform rituals and spells. If it is practical, I suggest that you do the same – try to see your whole house, or your part of it, as sacred space.

It has to be said that some magicians don't bother with sacred space and I think this is sad. They miss out on so much positive energy that would give any spell an added magical boost. You should also remember that creating sacred space acts as a connection between the mundane (your place of magic) and the world of the unseen (the astral plane). It is for this reason that the space inside the magical circle is known as being 'between the worlds'.

If you look around you, you will notice that sacred space is everywhere, in the man-made splendour of Stonehenge, and in a natural glade, wood or glen. Not far from where I live lies the beauty of Sherwood Forest, where the ancient trees simply ooze magic. The more you study the ambience and atmosphere of natural sacred space, the more you will be able to recreate it in your own home and your area of magic.

Sacred space is a power centre. It is where you 'plug yourself in' ready for action. This power is mobile and, provided you have requested as much, it can move with you wherever you go. Your magical circle is therefore especially effective as a form of protection ritual.

Creating sacred space

You should start by cleaning your magical area of all negativity in the following way.

Fill a small bowl or glass with water (spring water is best, but tap water will do fine). Now fill another small bowl with sea salt (this can be bought in most large supermarkets). Add three pinches of salt to the water and stir it in with your index finger. Next, moving in a clockwise direction, sprinkle the now magical water around your magical space. Concentrate especially on the area where the magical circle is to be cast. While you are performing this task, repeat this chant:

Outside of sorrow, outside of time,
Sacred space of magic – be mine!

Continue until you have covered the area. Pour the remaining water into the earth and leave the bowl of salt on your altar to continue absorbing any stray negative energies. You are now ready to begin casting your magical circle (see page 45) and working your rituals.

Keep this area free of negativity with regular cleansings, and do little things on a daily basis to keep the area feeling magical. This could be lighting a candle, the eternal flame (see page 139), or burning a stick of your favourite incense.

Candleburning altar

Central to your sacred space will be your candleburning altar. This should be a solid structure, preferably made of a fire-resistant material such as metal. If this is not possible then place your spell candles on a metal tea tray.

Most religions and spiritual practices make use of some sort of altar, whether it be the earth itself or a man-made construction. The altar is a place of power, peace and magic and it is here that you will be performing your candleburning rituals and spell castings. It is therefore important that you give yourself room to move and that the altar is large enough to be a serviceable working space.

Your altar is a vital part of your magical place, and sacred space will be constructed around it. This means that you will cast your circle around the altar – do not exclude it, it is part of your magic. On the altar you will place your spell candles, magical tools, magical figurines and any items you have that are specific to your own spiritual path. This could be a figure of Mary or Jesus, a

Bhudda, a depiction of a goddess or god, or a Star of David. If you do not follow any religion you could use instead a lovely picture of mountains or a waterfall.

When it comes to creating your altar, you have two main options. A table altar is ideal as it is sturdy and can be moved from place to place if necessary. It also gives you the best working space for candle magic. A wall altar, created by putting up two or three shelves, is convenient, however, if space is limited. This provides a perfect setting for displaying magical items, but you might find you need an additional space for working on.

If you decide upon a table altar, you will first need to position it correctly within your sacred space. Traditionally, the altar should be placed in the north or east of your magical circle. You can either use a compass to establish where north is, or you can work from the premise that north (twelve o'clock) is in front of you as you walk into the room, and south (six o'clock) is behind you. If your space is small, you may have to place the altar in another directional area altogether, and move the altar to the north or east for actual spell workings. If this is not possible, lay out your altar using the directions of a clock face, as above – the edge where you are sitting is south (six o'clock), and the edge opposite that is north (twelve o'clock).

It is preferable that your altar remains a permanent fixture within your magical place, but you could create an excellent altar using a folding table, the lid of the chest in which your tools are stored, or a large tea tray that slides easily under the bed when not in use.

Once you have decided where to place your altar, you need to choose the altar itself. To construct a table altar, you have a variety of choices. I use my dressing table as a working altar, and this is constantly set up with all my tools of the Craft. A friend of mine uses a small pine chest, which she pulls out into the middle of the room for use. Her space is limited, but she makes the most of it and has created a lovely little altar, which also serves as extra storage space. You could use a small coffee table, a chest, a dressing table, the top of a chest of drawers, a side board or a desk. You need not buy a special piece of furniture, but could use or adapt something you already have. Perhaps an old night stand or bedside table is hiding away in the attic, and needs only a clean and a coat of paint to make a beautiful altar. Look around you and use whatever you have handy.

If you choose to create a wall altar, you could construct this from shelves, a mantelpiece, a bookcase or an alcove. You could decorate the wall around this type of altar with magical symbols, pictures and wall decorations. Candle wall sconces would be ideal additions to a candleburning wall altar. Just use your imagination and be resourceful.

Once you have chosen the item that is to become your altar, clean it thoroughly and place it in your magical place. Now comes the fun bit – decorating it. Here you can let your imagination run wild. You might choose to paint your altar, to stencil it, or maybe to create a lovely embroidered altar cloth. Choose your colours carefully, and add ribbons, dried flowers and containers that match your colour scheme. Hang mobiles, plants and wind chimes above your altar and make it reflect who you are.

Although you are free to decorate your altar as you wish, there are some conventions to be followed when setting up a candleburning altar. At each side of the altar you should place a white candle in a tall candlestick. These will be your illuminator candles. Between these two candles you could place an item to reflect your spiritual beliefs as mentioned before or, if you do not follow any particular religion, you could use this area to put a vase of fresh flowers, a photograph, a beautiful crystal or an ornament of some sort. If you have an affinity with the ocean, then a collection of sea shells would be appropriate. An animal lover might put a small bowl of goldfish in this space. The choice is yours. Remember, this is your altar. It should speak to you of your magic and your power.

It is also traditional to have some representation of the four elements. These should be placed at the four corners of your altar. To represent earth you could use a rock, salt, crystals, a plant or a bowl of soil. Air could be represented by an incense holder and cones, a feather or a small statue of a bird. Fire could be a fiery-coloured crystal, a match, a sun-shaped ornament or a picture of a desert or a volcano. Water could be represented by a wishing well, a bowl of spring water, sea shells, a dolphin statue, a mirror or a postcard depicting the ocean's surge.

In the middle of the altar you should place a metal tea tray or an iron trivet. It is here that your spell candles will be left to burn. If you do not have room for a cupboard and bookcase in your magical place, then you will need a box or chest positioned near the altar in which to keep your spell candles and other magical materials, such as candle holders, coloured felt, cotton, ribbons, card and pens. You will also need an inscribing tool (a craft knife will do), parchment or good quality note paper (for making into spell papers), scissors and matches or a lighter. This is your spell box, where all your tools for effective candle magic will be ready to hand.

Your altar should always be clean and clear of dust so as to keep it free from negativity.

Pentacle

I strongly advise that you buy or make yourself a pentacle. This is a disc on which is inscribed the five-pointed star known as the pentagram. Although it is associated with witchcraft, it is used by all kinds of magical people for charging and empowering herbs, crystals, talismans and so on. You will need a pentacle for some of the spells in this book. They are available to buy from most occult stores, or you could make one yourself using modelling clay, or by drawing one on card and cutting it out. The magical power lies in the symbol itself, not in the material used.

CHAPTER 5

Mental preparation

Before making a start on your rituals, it is important to be in the right frame of mind, and there are a number of ways of achieving this: visualisation, centring, grounding and casting a magical circle. We shall look at the various ways of achieving this preparation in this chapter.

Visualisation

All magical people should learn the technique of visualisation. It is the force that brings the spell into manifestation, and for a spell to be effective, the spell caster must be able to 'see' the required result. Candles help to create a focus for the magical mind to work its will and thus aid visualisation.

Of all the techniques taught in this book, visualisation is probably the most important, because without it, your spells will fail. The human mind is an extraordinary tool and our most valuable asset. Whatever we can believe and accept as truth, we can create and bring into being. This gives us a tremendous power over life and a vital tool in magic.

To realise your dreams you must discover the power of visualisation. Without it, your dreams will be just that – dreams. Turning your dreams into reality is a very real possibility, but it requires you to be one hundred per cent committed to the manifestation of your goal, and to be totally convinced that your goal is achievable. Magic can help to take much of the pressure off, because by working regular spells, you are actually doing something positive towards your dream. And any magic performed will reaffirm your commitment towards that goal.

When performing candleburning rituals your visualisation must be strong and clear. You must see, with perfect clarity, all you want the spell to achieve. This means remaining entirely positive for the duration of the ritual. You must not allow doubt to creep into your mind and you must not be at all negative. This requires discipline, but if you truly want your spell to work, you will be able to leave all your doubts outside the circle.

Before you begin your candleburning ritual, go to a quiet area and relax. Take a few deep breaths and close your eyes. Now, imagine that you are standing on a beautiful beach. Walk down to the ocean and feel the water lapping at your feet. Ask the water to take away all your doubts, fears and negative thoughts. See these things as a detriment to your magic, for that is what they are. Feel all your doubts and negative energies travelling down your body and being pulled out through your feet. The ocean takes the negativity away and purifies it, bringing its waters back into balance with mind, body and spirit. You are left feeling light hearted and positive. Return back across the sand, leaving the waves crashing behind you. When you are ready, open your eyes and take three deep breaths. You are now ready to begin your magical working, having released anything that could prevent the manifestation of the spell.

During the spell casting, remain focused on only the positive outcome of your spell. Visualise yourself as having already achieved your magical goal, and imagine how this makes you feel. 'See' how you will react when manifestation of your magic occurs and know that you are one step closer to making your dream a reality. On completion of the spell, tell yourself that the ritual will work and your goal, whatever it is, is on its way to you. Now, once a day, just before you go to sleep, call the visualisation to mind and strengthen the spell.

Centring

When reading magical books or talking to magical people, you will come across the terms 'centring' and 'centred'. This is something that we all do naturally, yet magical people have made it into an art form. Centring helps to get the magical energies flowing together in synchronicity. It is a valuable skill to develop, and not just for use within the magical circle. When you are centred you will find that you can deal with stressful situations more calmly. Relaxation will become easier and you will feel very laid-back about everyday dramas, dilemmas and situations. People may even comment on how calm and collected you have become. A centred person is a powerful person, because they are in complete control of themselves.

If you feel nervous at the idea of centring, then help is at hand. As I said before, it is a totally natural practice. As an example, have you ever felt out of your depth, or as if you were going to pieces? Chances are that if you have felt this way, someone has said the words, 'pull yourself together'. What they are actually telling you to do is to become centred, to be in control and thus to feel much happier. The mental process of pulling all aspects of yourself back into line is what puts you back in control and makes you feel so much better. So if the term centring puts you off, use the phrase 'I'm going to pull myself together now'.

Before casting any magical spell it is important that you centre your energies. To do this, close your eyes and imagine your energy as coloured light or mist. At the moment, although this energy is enveloping you, it isn't really doing anything else. It is just there.

Now imagine that you are sucking this energy down from the top of your head and up from your toes. You are now 'pulling yourself together'. These energies meet at your solar plexus, which is just above your navel. In your mind's eye, shape this energy into a ball (use your hands if this helps). Now set the ball spinning steadily in a clockwise direction. You have now centred your energies and are ready to work magic and cast spells.

To begin with you may not notice any difference, but as you become more practised at centring, you will gradually realise how relaxed and calm you are and will feel much more balanced. Try to spend your whole day in a centred state. This will be difficult at first, but it will help if you perform the above exercise first thing in the morning, last thing at night, and any time in between when you feel stressed, angry, upset or tense. Gradually you will become more laid-back, even under pressure. This will create a sense of harmony, peace and balance in your life. Therefore magic will be easier to perform and goals will be that much more achievable.

Grounding

After working any form of magic, it is extremely important that you ground yourself. This means returning the magical energy to the earth. If we kept this energy lingering around us, we would be in a constant state of 'magical high'. The energy would then go off in all directions and would be wasted because it wasn't being properly directed.

Although most magical energy is released during the spell, some part of it just can't help clinging to the witch. This is the energy that needs to be grounded. We should send it back to the earth to heal her and do some good in the world. We can also ground the energy in a body of water.

So how do you go about grounding yourself after candle magic? Well, it is extremely likely that you already have the knowledge of grounding, you're just not aware of it. Think for a moment of a children's party. Lots of kids, lots of goodies and treats and, most importantly, lots of games. When I was a child, at every party I went to, the last game we played was called 'dead fishes'. In this game we would all lie flat on the floor and be as still as possible, and the last to move was the winner. It was a clever mum who thought this one up. With so much excitement and energy flying around between the children, 'dead fishes' is the perfect disguise for a grounding exercise. The high-voltage energy drains into the ground, the children calm down and parents stop tearing their hair out. A sense of peace and calm descends on all. This is grounding and there are many ways to do it.

Grounding can be either a physical or a mental exercise. Physical grounding can be done by lying flat on the floor or grass and letting the magical energy drain away into the earth. Alternatively you can place your hands flat on the bark of a tree, or the side of a rock face and let the energy drain through your hands.

To use water to ground the energy, you could take a shower. A bath is not recommended as the water you are soaking in will keep hold of the magical energy and you need it to drain away from you. Another way is to paddle in the sea or a stream and let the movement of the water pull the energy away from you. Or simply run your hands under the tap and rinse the energy away.

A mental grounding could be visualising yourself as a tree. Your legs are the trunk, your feet the roots and your head and arms are the branches. Allow the energy to drain down through the roots of this tree and so into the earth.

You should ground and centre after every spell you perform and then try to do something quiet for at least half an hour. Read a book, write a poem, watch a gentle film or listen to soothing music. Avoid anything that will upset your newly centred sense of calm and balance, or that will put you in a state of stress.

Casting a magical circle

All magic should be performed within a magical circle. This is the sacred space described earlier – the area devoid of negativity. The magical circle is an imaginary boundary and has been described by many as being 'between the worlds'. This means that the physical actions done within the circle on the mundane plane will be reflected back to you from the astral plane, the place of magic. This therefore effects the manifestation of the spell.

Constructed by the worker of magic before every spell, the magical circle works in two ways. To begin with, its boundary walls keep out any negative energies that are flying around so that your spell is not adversely affected by them. Secondly the circle will keep all magical energies and power raised within sacred space until you are ready to release them and set the magic free. The circle can also be used as a protective device and can be cast any time you are feeling frightened or vulnerable. It is an especially good practice to cast a circle around your home and around yourself. There are candle rituals for both these practices (see pages 123 and 122). As a magical person you will need to be able to cast a safe and secure circle under pressure and at any given time. But because the circle is a visionary exercise, there is no reason why you should not pick up this technique very quickly. It is important, however, that you practise the following circle casting until you have perfected it as an art form.

As with centring, there is no need to be worried about this exercise. The beauty of magic is that it utilises all the skills we already use on a daily basis – it just enhances them and makes us aware of our power. If you can see the face of your mother, or best friend, in your mind then you can cast an effective circle. If you can envision the burger you will have for lunch then you can cast an effective circle. If you spin out secret stories and plays in your head then you can cast an effective circle.

Often, newcomers to magic are a little put off by the fact that the circle itself cannot be seen with the physical eyes. They wrongly assume that because the circle is imaginary (for want of a better term) it is therefore unreal and pretend. Even worse, such people doubt the very existence of the magical circle on those grounds.

The circle is very real indeed, as any witch will tell you. It is as real as love, happiness, sound and the wind, all of which cannot be seen. We know that these things exist, however, because we feel them, and it is exactly the same with the magical circle. You will feel its existence around you. This awareness will increase over time as you become more skilled, but even in the beginning, you will feel the subtle energy you have cast. This will most likely manifest as a sense of confidence in your power, and it is up to you to make this stronger by reinforcing it with practice. Witches 'see' their circle with their third eye, or inner vision. If it helps to close your eyes in order to 'see' your circle, then by all means do so. And remember, this is a skill you use every day – you are simply directing it in a magical sense.

Before casting your circle you must centre your energies, as explained earlier. When you have done this, move to the centre of the room, close your eyes and stretch out your hand. Pointing with your index finger, turn slowly in a clockwise direction, pointing out a circle all around you. As you do so, envision a stream of brilliant blue light (rather like electricity) coming out from your finger and creating the circle. You are the centre of this circle and it is your own magical space.

Now imagine that this light expands both above and below you, passing unhindered through all physical objects. You are now standing at the heart of a sphere of blue light, as brilliant as lightning. Stamp your foot three times to dispel any lingering negativity. Your magical circle is now cast and you are ready to perform your chosen candleburning ritual.

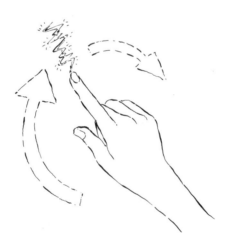

This is a very simple form of circle casting and it should not pose too much of a problem for the beginner. If you do find it difficult however, keep your eyes closed and repeat the process three times each day until you feel you are getting the hang of it.

Many magical people use more complicated methods of casting a circle and incorporate words of invocation. For candle magic this isn't really necessary and it is better in the beginning to keep things simple. Once you have practised and gained experience at circle casting you will be able simply to click your fingers and know instantly that your magical circle is there, protecting you and your rituals.

After working your spell, you must take down your circle. This is the time when your magic goes out into the universe to do your bidding, unless you have already released it as part of your spell. Taking down a circle is easy. Simply turn around in an anti-clockwise direction and imagine the blue light being drawn back into your hand. When this is done, clap your hands three times to disperse any last remnants of magical energy. You should then ground and centre yourself.

Practise casting and taking down your circle regularly, every day if you can. An amusing game is to cast a circle around yourself before going out for a walk. Then watch how many people literally walk around your magical boundary. Of course, they cannot see the circle, but they can sense it, and they know that the space within it is off limits to them. This has happened to me many times, and it is fun to see this outward proof of your power. Try it and see. The more people who avoid your circle, the more powerful it is.

Lastly, remember that all the techniques in this chapter are things that you subconsciously do on a daily basis. You are not learning a new skill – you are simply learning to be aware of what you already do and directing that skill towards your magic, thus increasing your power. Keep trying. I promise you'll get there in the end if you stick at it.

CHAPTER 6

Magical correspondences

Anything that can be used in conjunction with the spell candles in order to strengthen the ritual is known as a magical correspondence. We have already talked about moon phases and how the moon can affect the outcome of your magic. Here we will look at ways of enhancing the power of the candle by using such tools as herbs, trees, oils and crystals.

Choosing your correspondences depends entirely on what type of rituals you are performing and which items best suit your magical goal. For instance, when casting a money spell you might decide to use patchouli oil and dried mint. A love spell, however, would probably require two entirely different correspondences such as honey and rose petals, whilst a protection spell might call for a tendril of ivy and a protection incense. Each of the correspondences strengthens and supports the basic spell with its own unique qualities.

All this may sound a little complicated, but the correspondences given in this book are easily available. In fact, you may have many of them (such as honey and lemon juice) in your kitchen cupboards. The rest should be easily obtainable from the local supermarket, the garden, or on a walk through a nearby park or wood.

Most of the spells in this book require at least one item in addition to the candles themselves. This serves to strengthen the spell and give variety, making spell casting more fun and adding to your knowledge along the way. However, if you are pushed for time or money, then use the candle alone and reinforce your visualisation. Never put off working magic because you lack all the ingredients. Improvise with what you do have, or stick to a basic white candle and plenty of concentration. Remember that the magic is in you, not in the tools you use.

You will find, however, that by including such things as oils and crystals, you will make your spells more powerful because all the ingredients are working together towards the same end. Thus, manifestation may occur more quickly. Now, I'm not saying that you should load your money spell candle with every single herb that corresponds to prosperity, but by adding one or two, you are turning a basic spell into a ritual with three times the power.

Use the following lists if you find that you do not have the specified item for a particular spell and require a substitute. This is by no means a complete list of correspondences, but rather a collection of those that are readily available, and which you are most likely to have access to. As you become more experienced you may like to study this subject in greater depth and to experiment with different herbs and oils, or try different combinations. You will find that your magical power will grow with your experience and knowledge.

Correspondences for prosperity

Herbs: Mint, tea, bayberry, almond, cinnamon, patchouli.

Trees: Fir, pine, beech.

Oils: Peppermint, bayberry, patchouli, almond.

Crystals: Aventurine, jade, peridot, iron pyrites (fool's gold), loadstone, magnets.

Correspondences for passion

Herbs: Apple, cinnamon, clove, coriander, gardenia, ginger, jasmine, patchouli, rose, violet, ylang ylang.

Trees: Apple, elm, maple/sycamore.

Oils: Clove, jasmine, patchouli, rose, ylang ylang, lavender.

Crystals: Amethyst, rose quartz, carnelian, jasper.

Correspondences for power and protection

Herbs: Apple blossom, basil, bergamot, carnation, eucalyptus, lavender, nutmeg, rue.

Trees: Ivy, poplar, blackthorn, yew.

Oils: Eucalyptus, lavender, rose geranium.

Crystals: Tiger's eye, sodalite, azurite, blue lace agate, quartz.

Incense

You might also like to burn incense as part of your rituals. I strongly advise this as burning incense helps keep the magical area free from negativity. You do not necessarily have to use loose incense. You can buy cones or sticks in many of the fragrances listed above (such as lavender, geranium, rose, patchouli and pine) and so incense itself becomes a magical correspondence and part of the candleburning ritual.

Many occult stores sell incense that has been specially blended towards magical goals. These incenses have names like Money Drawing, Protection, Purification and so on. These are fine if you can get hold of them. If not, then use any stick of incense that is conducive to your magical goal.

CHAPTER 7

Candle power

The flame of a candle is perhaps the most beautiful and mystical of all magical tools. Today, candles are undergoing a revival and are again a fashionable item to have in the home. Most modern designers will incorporate a small collection of candles into the rooms they work on.

Most witches have candles burning around their home during the day and especially in the evening. As I write it is a hot summer's day and the light of the sun is everywhere. Yet I still have a candle burning on my desk that has been empowered with the gifts of creativity and free-flowing words, to aid me in the writing of this book. Barely a day goes by when I do not light a candle and work a spell of some sort.

Candle magic is actually a very ancient art and has been used as a part of ritual since the far-off days of the Roman Empire. In this chapter we will look at the basics of candle lore, so that you will be fully prepared to work on any of the spells laid out in the following chapters.

Magical candles come in a variety of colours and shapes, as you will see if you flick through any occult mail-order catalogue. There are seven-day candles, skull candles, human figure candles, cat and snake candles, and even candles shaped like male and female genitalia to aid with fertility spells. There are candles set in glass jars, traditional church candles, floating candles, knobbed candles, tea-lights and birthday candles, all of which can be used in your rituals. The list is endless. Each has its own magical purpose and can be very effective if the practitioner performs the spell correctly and remains entirely focused on the magical goal. These novelty candles are fun to use, and you will find spells using some of them in this book. However, they can be expensive and are not entirely necessary. Any ordinary candle will do. So if a spell calls for a black cat candle, and you do not have access to one, then feel free to use an ordinary black taper candle. Providing your visualisation and focus are strong, you should have no trouble manifesting your magical goal. Remember that the magic is in the person, not in the tools used.

Novelty candles are useful because they can automatically reinforce our focus. For example, if you felt you were having a run of bad luck and wished to break the cycle, an obvious choice of candle would be a black cat. Black cats are considered to be very lucky by magical people, and so such an association would automatically reinforce your focus of good luck and so help to break the pattern. But as mentioned before, never feel that you cannot work magic because you do not have all that a spell specifies. I cannot stress this enough. Those who wait for the perfect situation and the ideal set of tools will never work magic. If you know the value of improvisation, you will find you can work effective spells using whatever you have to hand.

Most old spells call for beeswax candles and these are generally considered to be the best because of their close association with nature. The bee itself is a symbol of industry and a rich and full life. Most people have heard of the expression 'drunk as a bee', meaning that while the bee is working hard for his queen, he is also deriving much pleasure for himself. Beeswax candles are considered essential by old spell books, but today they can be expensive and so are not compatible with regular spell casting. You may like to keep one or two in your magical candle box, but for most spells an everyday taper candle will be sufficient.

When buying candles make sure that they are free from cracks and are not broken in any way. A broken candle will break the power, as will a crack, and the spell could easily go awry. It is also better to buy loose candles, rather than boxed sets, as you can examine them carefully and make sure that they are in excellent condition. Also check the 'feel' of the candle. Is it hard or soft? Hard candles will be difficult to inscribe and softer wax is better for magical use. Store your spell candles in a box that is lined with a soft fabric to protect them. This could be as simple as an old shoe box with a piece of felt laid within, or a satin-lined wooden chest. Make sure this box is placed somewhere cool and out of direct sunlight – you would not want your candles to melt together on a hot sunny day.

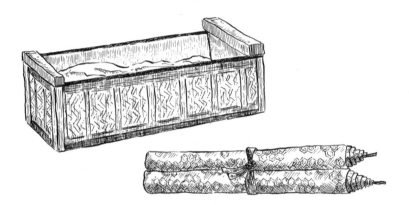

Make sure that you have plenty of good, solid candle holders. Choose ones that will hold the candle securely in an upright position so that the candle will not topple over when lit. Also, do not choose holders that are made of wood as they could be flammable. Be careful of glass holders as these can become uncomfortably hot and may crack. I had an experience once when a thin, frosted-glass candle holder literally shattered from the heat, leaving the flame exposed. Brass, pewter and metal are by far the best materials for holding spell candles, which may remain alight for many hours.

Some of the spells in this book use more than one candle, so you will need a few suitable candle holders. You need not buy them all at once, but somewhere between six and ten holders should be ample to make a start.

For novelty candles and large, fat candles, use the clay drainage saucers from terracotta plant pots, or a metal tray set on a trivet. Be careful with this one though, as the tray can get hot. When using metal holders on a wooden surface, use coasters to protect furniture from heat marks and scorching.

When using candles around the home, you are bound to have to deal with candle drippings from time to time. This used to be such a common problem that housekeepers had a very good method of dealing with it. Place a sheet of paper over the drippings and run it over with a warm iron, and the paper will absorb the warm wax and gently remove it from the altar cloth or furniture. I have tried this little trick myself and can vouch for its effectiveness.

If you decide to fragrance your candles with oil, you can enhance your spells in many ways, and to do this you will need a collection of essential oils. It is best to use pure essential oils rather than synthetic ones, as some synthetic oils are flammable and are therefore unsuitable for use in candle rituals. To identify oils, essential oils are always sold in dark glass bottles with a dropper in the neck. They tend to be a little more expensive than synthetic oils, but this is because they are pure and are not diluted with a carrier oil. A 5 ml bottle of essential lavender oil, which is one of the most readily available and cheapest oils, should cost around £4 in the UK, while a synthetic lavender oil may cost about £1. Synthetic oils are usually sold in clear glass bottles with labels that state they are for use in oil burners and to refresh pot pourri. If they state that they can be used in lamp rings, then they will withstand intense heat and therefore could be used for candle rituals, but is is preferable to use essential oils only. You will also need a carrier oil such as almond oil for use in your candle rituals.

For magical purposes it is essential that you perform only one spell on each candle. So, if your spell for banishment yesterday required you to let a black candle burn for one hour, and you still have half a black candle, you cannot use this particular candle for a different spell today. You could use it to repeat the same spell, thus reinforcing the original, but you cannot use it for a different magical purpose. In most cases candles are left to burn down, and if not, directions are usually given to bury the remainder of the candle in the earth, or float it in a living body of water.

Spell candles are always empowered for a particular purpose. Trying to use the same candle for two different goals goes against the magical grain and, in all likelihood, both spells will remain unsuccessful.

First rule of candle magic: Only one spell per candle.

The fourteen mystic shades

There has been much debate over colour correspondences and how they should be used in magical spell casting. My own theory is that if a particular colour works for you in some way, you should use it, regardless of what various books say. For instance, if purple speaks more strongly to you of love than any other colour, then by all means go with purple. It is your spell after all, and providing you visualise with clarity, there is no reason why it should not work. In this book you will find suggested colours for each spell. In the beginning it may be wise to stick with these, but as you become more experienced, feel free to experiment with other colours and different combinations.

Below are black, white and the twelve mystic shades, colour correspondences which have stood the test of time and which I use personally and have found to be effective.

Silver: For spells of femininity, moon power and the night.

White: For purity, cleansing, childhood, innocence, truth and protection.

Gold: For masculinity, sun power and the daylight hours.

Yellow: For communication, creativity, psychic ability, attraction, examinations and tests.

Green: For finance, security, employment, career, fertility and luck.

Light blue: For calmness, tranquillity, patience, understanding and good health.

Blue: For healing, wisdom, knowledge, dream interpretation and dreamscaping (using your dreams in a magical way to solve problems, find answers and so on).

Pink: For honour, friendship, virtue, morality, success and contentment.

Purple: For power, mild banishings, ambition, inner strength, business success and physical fitness.

Orange: For adaptability, a zest for life, energy and imagination.

Brown: For neutrality, stability, strength, grace, decision making, pets and family issues.

Red: For all love aspects and courage in adversity.

Grey: For cancellations, anger, greed and envy.

Black: For strong banishings, bindings, limitations, loss, confusion and defining boundaries.

This is by no means the last word on colour correspondences for candleburning rituals, and as with anything else, you must form your own opinions as to whether this list seems right for you personally. All the spells in this book adhere to these mystic shades, and all I can say is that they have always worked for me.

Second rule of candle magic: Use the colour you feel is most conducive to your magical goal.

Making candles

In ancient times, creating fire was considered to be the most magical of arts and those skilled in this craft were believed to have been specially chosen by divinity. Making your own candles can be a fulfilling magical hobby. More importantly, if you do decide to make your own spell candles, you can add specific herbs and oils to make the candle more truly representative of your magical goal. In making a prosperity candle for example, you could add cinnamon, mint and patchouli oil, creating the entire spell within that one candle. Of course, making your own candles is not essential for effective candle magic, but it is important that you are aware this door is always open to you, particularly if you are having difficulty obtaining a specific type of spell candle. There are many candle-making kits on sale, and you could begin with one of these. Alternatively, you could melt down some plain white kitchen candles or save small stumps of other household candles (remove the wicks first). To colour the candles, use a commercial candle dye, or simply add a couple of wax crayons.

Begin by grating the wax and putting it in a medium-size, deep pan. Put this pan into a larger pan of boiling water in order to heat the wax. This is the process cooks use when melting chocolate as it provides a gentle heat.

If you are going to add herbs and spices, you should grind these to a fine powder with a mortar and pestle. Do this whilst the wax is melting. Once all the candle wax is liquid, add the colour or the unwrapped wax crayons and continue to heat gently. Stir in the colour to create an evenly distributed shade. Do not allow the wax to harden – keep the heat at a reasonable level to prevent this. Now add any herbs and oils and state the purpose of this magical mixture (be it prosperity, protection, banishment). Smell the fragrance of the wax to ensure you have used enough oil. If not, add a little more. Only essential oils should be used for this job. Now take a length of wick and dip it into the melted wax. Hold it up and allow a thin coat of wax to dry thoroughly before dipping it again. Continue to dip until you have a properly formed candle of a reasonable thickness. The dipping will become easier as the candle becomes thicker and heavier.

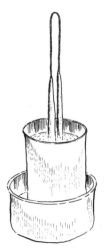 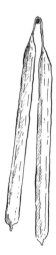

Next you must leave the candle to harden and dry, by hanging it in a safe place. An airing rack is ideal, or you could peg your candles out on the washing line. When your candle is completely dry and has firmed up nicely, cut off the bottom to make it straight so that it will sit properly in its candle holder. Your spell candle is now ready to use in ritual.

Making beeswax candles

Beeswax candles are not as readily available as other candles and they tend to be more expensive, although you can usually buy them in New Age shops and often in farm shops. If you are going to make your own candles, you can simply add a teaspoon or so of honey to your melting mixture to achieve a similar result.

If you feel that candle dipping is beyond your means or capabilities, then all you need are some plain candles and a jar of honey. These candles should only be created if they are to be used immediately. You cannot store them. You would have to find real beeswax candles if you wanted to keep them for any length of time. Take the candle and, using a blunt knife, smear a thin layer of honey over the candle's surface. Lift the candle to your nose and see if you can detect the fragrance of honey. If you can't, then add a little more. Once the candle has been coated with honey, place it in a holder and light the wick. As the candle burns, the sweet fragrance of honey will pervade your home and bring the magic of nature indoors.

This candle is exceptionally good for all types of cleansing ritual, and for spells of home peace and tranquillity. It is also a good candle to keep on your altar as a 'perpetual flame', or to place on an altar dedicated to the home devas and hearth spirits.

Charging candles

In magic, to 'charge' or 'empower' means to instil an object with its magical power and your own personal power, thus creating an effective magical tool. All your spell candles must be charged or empowered before use. This process works to align the candles with your magical goal. There is a slight difference between the charging and empowering processes, but each essentially does the same thing. They convert the candle from an ordinary piece of wax and wick, into a tool of magic.

To charge a candle, or any other magical component, you will need the pentagram star mentioned earlier. If you do not have a pentacle, then draw a five-pointed star on a sheet of paper or card, and using a pair of compasses, surround the star with a circle. Cut out the circle and you have a home-made pentacle that will serve for all your charging needs.

Place the pentacle in the centre of your candleburning altar. Now take a small slip of paper and write upon it your magical goal. Let's say that you write the word 'prosperity'. Now take the slip of paper and wrap it around the middle of the candle. Tie it with thread and place the whole thing on the pentacle.

The pentagram is a very powerful symbol and it exudes magic, no matter what its basic material. By placing the spell candle on the pentacle, the magic will be absorbed by the candle and directed to the magical goal by the word printed on the slip of paper. You should add to this invisible process by visualising your goal as strongly and clearly as you possibly can. When you feel the time is right, take up the candle, remove and burn the slip of paper, and begin to work your candleburning ritual.

You do not have to be present for the whole of the charging process – you can visualise your goal wherever you are. This means that you can leave your spell candles charging while you go out, clean the house, take a bath or even when you go to bed. The candle will be charging from your energies around the altar and the power of the pentacle, and will be ready for use when you come back to it.

Empowering candles

Empowering an object is done in a slightly different way. For this process, you should take the candle and hold it firmly between both palms. Close your eyes and begin to chant a mantra of your magical goal. For instance, you could chant:

I empower this candle with the gift of love – bring me love.

To empower something means to instil it with your own energy and personal power. You personally direct your own power towards the magical goal. Empowering a candle can be done as you are anointing it with oil, or inscribing it with words and symbols. In this way, you can save yourself time by doing two jobs at once.

Dressing candles

Anointing a spell candle with oil is known as 'dressing' the candle. Adding oils and herbs to your magical candles is a delightful way to enhance their power. Such spell candles really do create an aura of magic around them as the various fragrances rise up into the air as the candle burns. They are a beautiful addition to any magical altar, shrine or space-clearing exercise.

If you decide to add an oil to your ritual, it is important to choose carefully. The oil must be in tune with your magical goal. Use the list of correspondences for assistance in choosing the correct herbs and oils (see pages 50–1). Essential oils are the best kind for this purpose (see page 56), but if you do use synthetic oils only use one that states it is suitable for lamp rings.

To prepare oil in which to dress your candles, dilute a few drops of your chosen essential oil in about 15 ml/1 tbsp of a carrier oil such as almond oil.

For spells that draw something towards you, you should begin at the wick and rub the oil downwards to the centre of the candle. Then turn the candle and begin at the bottom, and again rub the oil towards the centre of the candle. This pulls the power to you from all directions, making manifestation much easier.

For spells that remove something from your life, begin at the centre of the candle and rub the oil outwards in both directions, to the top and the bottom of the candle. This ensures that the negative energy is pulled away from you on all levels.

If you prefer, you can pour a few drops of essential oil into a bottle cap and apply to the candle with a small paintbrush.

To add herbs to your work, simply sprinkle the dried herbs on to a sheet of newspaper, then roll the anointed candle over the herbs several times until it is evenly covered. Note that the candle must first have been anointed with oil in order for the herbs to stick. Your candle is now ready to light.

Inscribing candles

Many workers of magic choose to inscribe their candles with words or symbols. To inscribe your candle you will need a suitable tool such as a craft knife. Think of a word or symbol that signifies your magical need, such as a heart for love, or the amount of money you need inscribed in figures.

Once again, to bring this need towards you, inscribe from the wick downwards. To remove anything negative, inscribe from the bottom of the candle upwards.

Inscribing candles is often used as an alternative to candle dressing, though personally I feel that the most powerful candles are those that have been both inscribed and dressed. This is, however, a personal choice and you must feel free to use whichever method suits you. If you choose to use the inscribing and dressing methods together, then do your inscribing first.

Creating spells

'You mean I get to write my own spells?' Of course you do! What's the point of being a magical person if you cannot create your own spells and rituals as and when you need them?

The most powerful spells you will ever work are the ones that you create yourself. Remember to be the master of your own magic and to take full control and responsibility for your spell castings.

Creating your own spells is a fun, rewarding and empowering experience. And anything that empowers us can only be a good thing. It isn't difficult to write your own spells, although this aspect of magic comes with the most responsibility. You are not on your own, however. There are many books of magic and spells on the market, some better than others, it has to be said. Use these texts to create a backbone for your own creations.

Remember the ethics of magic and abide by them. Check and double check any words used to make sure they 'harm none'. And as a safety precaution, finish all spells with the words:

I cast this spell with harm to none.

Check that your magical correspondences are correct, and that your incantations are clear and precise. Magical words do not have to rhyme, but it is better if they do. For one thing a rhyme is easier to remember. You do not have to be Tennyson, Keats or Shakespeare, just make sure that you say what you mean – and mean what you say.

Remember that you can adapt any spell by changing the colours and correspondences used. For example, changing a red love candle to a black candle would change a love spell into a banishing spell. Such adaptations are yours to make if you cannot find a spell to suit your need. But you must also remember to work at an alternative moon phase and to write your own appropriate chants and incantations.

And that's basically all there is to it! Use this book as your guide. Study the construction of the spells, look carefully at correspondences and the words used. Most of all use your intuition and common sense. If you feel your spell may harm someone – don't do it. Re-word and re-write until it is gentle, yet at the same time focused, directed and powerful.

Over the following chapters you will find a wealth of spells and rituals that will enrich your life and aid you in self-transformation. Be the best that you can be, face everything with courage, and let the magic begin ...

CHAPTER 8

Flames of passion

Love is perhaps the purest and most turbulent of emotions – from the fragility of a blossoming romance to the heart-rending, icy chill of rejection; from the heights of passion and ecstasy to the birth of a child to seal the bond. Love has many faces and is a universal language. Every age and all cultures know the joys and sorrows of love, and as a subject it has been the inspiration for artists, writers and poets alike. One cannot possibly count the number of words that have been written in the name of love. Novels, poems, screenplays and letters all have Cupid's arrow firmly lodged within them.

There is no doubt that love holds a certain magic of its own. But what if that magic could be harnessed and directed to the source of your desire? Imagine what that would mean. You could attract your ideal, your dream lover into your life.

Love is a very special feeling, one to be nurtured and caressed. Love is sacred and the spells and rituals of this chapter will help you to draw the wonderful experience of love into your life.

As with all other forms of magic, love spells have a set of rules that should be strictly adhered to. There are many different types of love spell, and they don't just apply to romantic love either. Love spells can be used to enhance and strengthen all kinds of relationship such as those with friends, neighbours, teachers, co-workers, parents, siblings and other family members. Love rituals can even be cast so that you can better understand and connect with your pet.

On the flip side of the coin, love spells can be turned around and reversed. This sends the power in the opposite direction. Such spells can be used to deter unwanted admirers, to help to remove yourself from a destructive relationship, or to ease the pain of a break-up or divorce.

When casting love spells, you should tread very carefully and consider whether your spell will bring about the best outcome for all those involved. This is of vital importance. You must not act selfishly when working love magic, though the temptation to do so may be great. Spells to make a man or woman leave his or her spouse are a definite no-no. Rest assured that if you are meant to be with someone, you will be. It may, however, happen gently and gradually, in the same way that one season changes to another.

You must also ensure that your spell does not interfere with another person's free will. This basically means that you cannot cast a spell with a particular person in mind, because that would be altering their free will and therefore falls under the realm of 'dark magic'. (You will find no dark spells in this book, only those that are gentle in nature and follow the 'harm none' rule.) Instead, you should imagine the qualities of your ideal mate. If you name a particular person, you could end up marrying Mr or Miss Wrong, live through ten years of hell, and completely miss an opportunity with Mr or Miss Right. It is far better to imagine your ideal than a specific person. 'But,' you say, 'my ideal is a knight in shining armour and they don't exist any more!' This is true, but think instead of your knight's qualities: truthfulness, honour, valour, sensitivity, respect for people, and so on. Now you have the essence of the fantasy. And the essence is very real indeed, so cast a spell with those knightly qualities in mind, and you may well realise your fantasy with someone in the real world.

When it comes to love magic, binding spells are out – no ifs, no buts, no maybes. This means that you cannot use magic to bind another person to you, no matter what. No matter how much you love them, no matter how much they love you, no matter how totally convinced you are that this is 'it', this is 'the one', this is going to last forever. If all that is true, then it hardly needs a binding spell.

Why is it unethical to bind a love with magic? To answer this question, we need to look at the potential effects of such a spell. In binding a person to you, you are taking away that person's free will. As a result your partner will undoubtedly 'feel' bound to you, as opposed to choosing to be with you. Of course they cannot get away, because of the binding, so they will seek other ways to 'escape'. They may begin to drink heavily, experiment with drugs, spend more time at work than they do at home, or embark on a string of affairs. Meanwhile, you're wondering what's gone wrong. You're desperately unhappy and want only to put an end to the relationship. But something always stops you and now you're both left feeling trapped and miserable. If you do eventually split, there is a strong chance that it will be a long drawn-out and difficult process. That's binding. Don't do it. There are other, gentler ways to strengthen a love bond and you will find them in this chapter.

As always, you must make absolutely sure your spell is cast with harm to none.

Creating a true love shrine

An altar dedicated to love is a valuable component in love magic, and can be used as an extremely effective magical tool. As you now know, any altar is a place of power, so your candle rituals of passion will be particularly potent when cast at your love altar. Such an altar can also act as a constant reminder of your intentions, be they a romantic involvement, family affection or even self-love.

Most types of spell can be cast at your candleburning altar, so you could adapt your existing altar to construct a love shrine on a temporary basis. Better still you could create a separate altar dedicated to the love goddess and her gifts. My own home is full of little altars and shrines, each with its own particular use. I find that this enhances my personal space and is conducive to magical living. These places may not look like altars to non-magical people, but that is what they are none the less. They are places of power.

The first step in creating your love shrine is to choose a suitable surface. Now drape this surface with a beautiful piece of red velvet, silk or felt. No matter what kind of love you would like to enhance or bring into your life, your true love shrine must begin with the essence of self-love, as without this acceptance of yourself, you will never get anyone else to accept you fully. This could be represented with the central placing of a pink candle, or an oil burner in which you burn your favourite fragrance. You should then use some representation of spirit and divine love. This could be a passage from your holy book or a depiction of the god or goddess of your religion. My own favourite way of representing divinity is to use a statue of an angel. The sight of an angel immediately speaks to us of divinity, goodness and unconditional love. And of course, angels transcend all religious boundaries. They are universal messengers of love, so who better than an angel for a love shrine?

Another technique is to dedicate your altar to a goddess or god of love. For example, you might cover your altar with pictures and statues of cherubs to represent the Roman god Cupid. Or you might place a figure of the goddess Venus in the centre of your altar and surround her with candles and scallop shells.

Use your true love shrine to display anything that speaks to you of love. A photograph of family, friends or a beloved pet would remind you that you are not alone. Heart-shaped trinket boxes can be used to keep spell papers in. Containers made from sea shells

would be particularly appropriate as these represent Venus, who came from the sea. Heart-shaped jewellery, love spoons, turtle doves and your grandmother's antique lace wedding veil, all have a place on a love shrine. The idea is to make such a strong representation of love that this finer feeling cannot help being attracted to you.

Personally I think nothing looks quite so lovely on a love altar as a crystal vase filled with red and pink roses. These will bring life to your shrine, and will act to bring both romantic love and friendship or family love into your life. They also serve as a reminder of the generous love of mother nature, who endlessly supplies us with fruit, flowers, grains and vegetables to ensure our survival. Other flowers and plants you may like to use on your altar are forget-me-nots, pansies (also called heartsease), bluebells and wreaths of holly and ivy, which represent the unity of masculine and feminine and are especially attractive around yule-tide when flowers are scarce. In these plants, beauty and symbolism combine to give a really positive message.

If you are in an established relationship, a beautifully framed photograph of the two of you together should have a place of honour on your true love shrine. You could add to this any valentine cards you have from your partner, or any love letters, prettily tied with a red ribbon. Old theatre and cinema tickets or other reminders of your first date and special outings should also be put on your altar to attract even more happy times through the magic of memories.

If you are not in a relationship right now and would like to work magic to attract someone, then your love shrine will be slightly different. Do not put a photograph of yourself alone on the altar as this sends out the wrong message to the universe. Instead, feel free to add a photo of yourself and a friend or family member, or even a picture of you and your pet. This will remind you of the love you are already given and already share. By acknowledging the gifts we already have, we attract more into our lives. Remember, like attracts like. Be thankful for what you have and you will have more to be thankful for.

To bring romantic love into your life, decorate your altar with red candles, rose petals, pictures and figurines of loving couples, a book of love poetry and maybe even a 'wanted' ad that you have created describing your ideal partner. And yes, I suppose if you really must, you can add that picture of a knight in armour or a fair damsel, providing, of course, that the picture is of a fantasy nature and does not depict an actual person.

Remember that you can change your altar to correspond to the seasons. This shows that you are willing to work your magic in harmony with the universe, rather than working against it. Begin by adding seasonal flowers and fruits such as tulips, bluebells, pansies and painted eggs in spring. Roses, foxgloves, sweet peas and a dish of strawberries can be used in summer. To represent autumn, add poppies and wheat, fallen leaves of autumnal hues and a basket of blackberries, and in winter, place holly, ivy, mistletoe, acorns and pine cones on your love altar. Apples are a very magical fruit and are also considered to be the fruit of love. They are also appropriate as an altar decoration at any time of the year and are used in many love spells. As the fruit is so readily available, the spells can be cast regularly to bring very positive results to love and relationships.

Love oil candle dressing

Purpose of ritual: To create an oil suitable for all love spells.

Items required: Almond oil, lavender oil, rose geranium oil, ylang ylang oil, bowl, dark glass bottle, rose petals (optional), label, pen.

Suggested lunar phase: Full moon.

We have already stated that a candle dressed in oil is a very powerful tool. Whilst you can use any of the essential oils listed as correspondences to love magic, you can also make a dressing oil using a blend of oils and empowering it specifically towards attracting love into your life. This oil can then be used as a dressing for any candles and spell papers you use when working love magic.

To begin with you will need a small amount of almond oil. Between a quarter and half a cup will be sufficient. Add to this three drops of lavender oil, three drops of rose geranium oil and three drops of ylang ylang oil. All these should be pure essential oils, not the synthetic perfumed variety (see page 56). Stir these oils together with your finger and as you do so, concentrate on bringing all forms of love into your life – romantic love, family love, friendships, and the love received from pets. When you feel ready, transfer the oil into a dark glass bottle. If you like you can then add two or three rose petals to the magical mixture. Lastly, label the bottle 'love oil dressing' and store it in a cool, dark place, away from direct sunlight. Your oil is now ready to use in any of your love spells.

Wax talisman of love

Purpose of ritual: To attract love into your life.

Items required: Red candle, greaseproof paper, love oil, dried rosemary, knitting needle or pencil, craft knife, narrow red ribbon.

Suggested lunar phase: Waxing moon.

Talismans have been used for centuries for all sorts of magical goals and purposes. Here, you are going to make one that is dedicated to love.

Sit at your altar and light the red candle. Focus completely on attracting romantic love into your life. Once the flame has taken hold, pick up the candle and begin to drip wax on to a small sheet of greaseproof paper. When you have a pool of melted wax, add a single drop of love oil candle dressing and a small pinch of dried rosemary. Whilst the wax is still malleable, place a hole in the top of it using a knitting needle or pencil. Then you can either mould the wax into a heart shape, or wait until the wax has hardened and inscribe a heart on to it. Finally, thread a narrow piece of red ribbon through the hole at the top, and either carry the talisman with you or hang it on your love shrine.

Wax talisman of friendship

Purpose of ritual: To enhance old friendships and attract new ones.

Items required: Pink candle, greaseproof paper, lavender oil, dried lavender heads, mortar and pestle, knitting needle or pencil, craft knife, narrow pink ribbon.

Suggested lunar phase: Waxing moon.

This talisman is made using the same procedure as the spell on page 74. As you light the candle, you should focus on friendship. Once you have made a pool of melted pink wax, add a single drop of lavender oil and a pinch of dried lavender heads that you have ground with a mortar and pestle. Once again, place a hole through the top of the talisman and inscribe or fashion the wax into a flower shape. Thread a narrow piece of pink ribbon through the hole at the top and your talisman is ready to hang wherever you like.

Talisman tree

Purpose of ritual: To create a spell tree for all your talismans.

Items required: Vase, fallen twigs; ribbons, braids, gold or silver paint, glitter (all optional).

Suggested lunar phase: Full moon.

Wax talismans are simple to make and their magic is very effective. You can dedicate them to virtually any magical goal or purpose, and can make more than one talisman for the same purpose, hanging them in various places around the house, in the car and so on. A nice idea though, is to create a talisman tree.

Find or buy a pretty vase and go out into the garden or for a walk and collect fallen twigs. When you have a fair-sized bunch of twigs, arrange them neatly in the vase and place the whole thing on your candleburning altar. Now hang your wax talismans from the branches of your talisman tree. You may like to go further and decorate the branches with ribbons and braids, or you could spray them with gold or silver paint and sprinkle them with glitter while the paint is still wet. Use your imagination and make your talisman tree a thing of beauty as well as power.

Apple pip love spell

Purpose of ritual: To decide between suitors.

Items required: White candle, oil of your choice, apple pips.

Suggested lunar phase: Full moon.

This spell is an effective form of divination and will help you to make a choice between possible partners.

First, dress the candle with oil, moving from both ends to the centre of the candle. The oil can be an essential oil of your choice, love oil candle dressing, or plain almond oil.

Next, take as many fresh apple pips as you have suitors and stick them in a line around the candle, naming each pip for one of your suitors as you do so. Now light the candle and watch to see which pip falls first. The last pip to fall from the candle is the suitor you should choose.

Fruits of love candle holders

Purpose of ritual: To bring romantic love into your life.

Items required: Red candle, bright, shiny red apple, apple corer, sharp knife, trivet.

Suggested lunar phase: Waxing moon.

This is a fun way to enhance your candle spells using the fruits of love – apples. Take out enough of the core of the apple so that you can place a red candle in it securely. Now take a sharp knife and inscribe the word 'love' on to the body of the candle. Put the candle into the hole and place the whole thing on a trivet on your altar. Light the candle and then sit before your altar meditating on the love you already enjoy and the love you wish to bring into your life. After a few minutes, snuff out the candle. Repeat this process for the next six days. On the final day of the spell, allow the candle to burn right down and then bury the apple in the garden or somewhere very near your home.

Love apple lanterns

Purpose of ritual: To light the way to love.

Items required: Small pink birthday candle, shiny, red apple, sharp knife, love oil.

Suggested lunar phase: Waxing moon.

To make love apple lanterns you will again need a shiny, red apple. Cut off the top of the apple and begin to scoop out the core and much of the flesh. This can be tricky but it is worth persevering with. Once you have hollowed out the apple, take a small pink birthday candle and dress it with love oil. Light this candle and drip the hot wax into the apple, then quickly press the birthday candle into the pool of wax. Place the apple lantern on your true love shrine and concentrate your power on manifesting love. Now take the top of the apple and the hollowed out flesh and put it outside for the birds in a selfless act of love. Allow the apple lantern to burn itself out and then bury it in the garden.

Twelve hearts love spell

Purpose of ritual: To enhance an established relationship.

Items required: Red candle, red paper or card, scissors, pen, rose oil, red thread, needle.

Suggested lunar phase: Full moon.

Begin by cutting twelve hearts out of deep red paper or card. Write your own name on six of these hearts and your lover's name on the other six. Now take a red candle and begin to dress it with rose oil. Think of your lover as you gently rub the oil into the wax until the candle is covered and evenly scented.

Set the candle in a holder at the centre of your love altar and call upon Venus, goddess of love, asking that she help you and your lover become more in tune with one another, that you may form a closer, more romantic bond of love. Place the twelve hearts in a circle around the red candle, alternating the names. Now light the candle in the name of love and Venus. Sit quietly for a while, watching the flame and meditating upon your love for your partner. Breathe in the fragrant rose oil and relax, allowing yourself to spin happy day-dreams of your future together. Now thread the needle with the red cotton, and slowly and methodically pass the needle through the centre of each heart. Work your way around the candle beginning in the south (six o'clock), the direction of love. When all the hearts are joined together, remove the needle and wrap the remaining cotton around the hearts, binding them more closely. Take up the candle and carefully drip hot wax on to the end of the thread to seal the bond.

Put the candle back on the love altar and allow it to burn down naturally. Give thanks to Venus for her assistance and place the twelve paper hearts beneath your bed to work their magic.

To attract your ideal lover

Purpose of ritual: To attract your ideal mate.

Items required: One red and one white candle, craft knife, strong thread.

Suggested lunar phase: Waxing moon.

Go to your love altar and sit quietly for a while, thinking about the qualities you would wish for in an ideal mate. Take hold of the white candle and inscribe it with your name. Place this in the centre of your altar. Now inscribe a question mark on the red candle, and place this at the far left of the altar.

Next take a piece of strong thread, the length of which is just slightly longer than the distance between the two candles. Tie the ends of the thread to the candles, thus forming a connection. Now light the white candle and say:

I light this candle, blessed be. Bring the one who's right for me.

Light the red candle and once again concentrate on the qualities of your ideal mate. Next, gently turn the white candle 360 degrees, so that the cotton is wrapped around the base. Be very careful as you do this and steady both candles with your hands. By turning the white candle, the red candle will have been drawn a little closer to its mate. Then snuff out both candles. Repeat this procedure every day until the candles are standing side by side. At this point you should allow the candles to burn down. Know that your ideal lover is on the way to you.

A spell to overcome shyness

Purpose of ritual: To release feelings of timidity and shyness.

Items required: Purple candle, ylang ylang oil, mortar and pestle, dried violet petals, sheet of paper, candle holder, greaseproof paper, knitting needle or pencil, craft knife, narrow ribbon.

Suggested lunar phase: Full moon.

This is a useful spell for those of you who are timid with members of the opposite sex. A purple candle is used to represent power. Take the candle and dress it with a strong fragrance such as ylang ylang. Now, with a mortar and pestle, grind up some dried violet petals (these can be bought ready dried from herbalists, or you can dry the flowers yourself). Once the petals have been ground to a fine powder, empty them on to a sheet of paper and roll the candle over them until it is evenly covered. Set the candle in a holder and light it, visualising yourself with total confidence and self assurance. Allow the candle to burn until it is approximately two to three centimetres (about one inch) tall.

Now take this candle stub and use it to make a talisman of confidence, following the instructions given previously on wax talismans (see pages 74–5). Inscribe on it a symbol of boldness such as a sword or a forward-pointing arrow (pointing upwards towards the top of the talisman). Carry this talisman with you and repeat the spell every full moon, adding the old talisman to your talisman tree, and carrying the new one. Gradually you will feel yourself overcoming shyness and acting with confidence and positivity.

To take love into yourself

Purpose of ritual: To absorb fully the essence of love.

Items required: Red candle, apple, knife, love oil.

Suggested lunar phase: Waxing moon.

This is another apple and candle spell. Peel the apple, and keep the peel as you will be using it later. Dress the red candle with love oil candle dressing, and empower it with love by holding it between your palms and saying:

> *I empower this candle with the gift of love.*
> *This is my will – bring me love.*

Now set the candle at the centre of your love altar and light the wick. Next take up the apple, and using a sharp knife, carve a love heart into its flesh. Now say:

> *I name this apple fruit of love and I take love into myself.*

As the candle burns, eat the apple, concentrating as you do so on your magical goal. Eat the apple right down to the core, then wrap the core in the apple peel and bury it all in the earth. Allow the candle to burn down completely. Know that your spell will work and love will come to you.

A Hallowe'en candle ritual

Purpose of ritual: To bring love to your life within twelve moons.

Items required: Tea-light candle, medium to large pumpkin, sharp knife.

Suggested lunar phase: Not applicable, perform on All Hallows' Eve.

Hallowe'en, known as Samhain to witches, is one of the most magical nights of the year. It is certainly the night most associated with magic and witchcraft, and it would be a shame not to take advantage of its power.

Cut off the top of the pumpkin and hollow out the middle. Take a sharp knife and, instead of carving out a scary face, carve your pumpkin with random love hearts. This may be a little tricky, but persevere as the spell is well worth it. Now light your tea-light candle and carefully place it into the pumpkin. Hold your hands over the pumpkin and repeat the following chant three times:

> *On this night of All Hallows' Eve,*
> *I ask that true love I shall receive.*
> *Let me dance to a lover's tune,*
> *This spell takes effect by the twelfth full moon.*

Place the pumpkin on your love altar and allow the tea-light to burn out. Alternatively you could make several of these love pumpkins and dot them around the house, thus filling your home with the light of love.

Reflective love spell

Purpose of ritual: To attract love.

Items required: Red candle (for romance) or pink candle (for friendship), hand mirror.

Suggested lunar phase: Full moon.

Place the candle on the altar and light it. Concentrate your personal power on the manifestation of your magical goal. Now hold the mirror behind the candle and position it so that the flame is reflected on to your face. Repeat the following chant nine times:

The light of love shines on me. This is my will, so mote it be.

Carry out this procedure every day until the candle has burned down. Try to remain positive about your magical goal as this will help to speed up manifestation.

To choose between suitors

Purpose of ritual: To make a choice using magic.

Items required: White candles (as many as you have suitors).

Suggested lunar phase: Waning moon.

Name each candle after a suitor – you may like to carve a name or an initial into the candles but you do not need to dress them with any oils. Stand the candles in a row and light them from the same flame (a taper or lighter). Now watch and see which candles burn out first. You do not have to stand over them constantly, but keep your eye on them. The candle that dies last is named for your true love and that person should be your choice.

Queen of hearts spell

Purpose of ritual: To become popular with the opposite sex.

Items required: Red candle, queen of hearts card (king of hearts if you are male), pen, love oil, candle holder.

Suggested lunar phase: Waxing moon.

If you would be a queen of hearts, take this card from the deck and write your name in all four corners. This ensures your ability to attract from all directions. Next, rub the card with love oil candle dressing and put it face up in the centre of your love shrine. Now take the red candle and dress this with love oil too. As you do so, empower the candle with the powers of attractiveness and desirability. Visualise yourself surrounded by adoring suitors. Next, put the candle in a holder and place this on top of the card and light the wick. As the candle burns it will enhance your ability to attract the attention of men.

Be warned though, if you don't like to be the centre of attention, or would feel hounded if pursued, this spell is not for you.

For the love of a pet

Purpose of ritual: To form a strong connection with your pet.

Items required: Brown candle, photograph of your pet, candle holder, if possible some hair, or feathers, from your pet (naturally shed, not plucked), almond oil.

Suggested lunar phase: Waxing moon. For a new pet, use the new moon.

To begin with you will need a photograph of your pet. Place this beneath the candle holder and concentrate your power on blessing the friendship with your pet, letting love, trust and understanding flow between you, aiding easy companionship. If your pet species has a particular guardian deity you would like to use, then by all means call on them by name (for example, you could call upon the Egyptian cat goddess, Bast).

Dress your candle with almond oil and stick the hair or feathers around the base of the candle. Concentrate hard on your magical goal and light the candle. See yourself and your pet sharing many happy years of love and companionship together. If practical, have your pet on your knee (though safely away from the flame) at this time and gently stroke and croon to him or her as the candle burns. Allow the candle to burn down completely.

Beauty spell

Purpose of ritual: To increase beauty.

Items required: One red candle, one candle the colour of your skin, one candle the colour of your hair and one the colour of your eyes, love oil.

Suggested lunar phase: Full moon.

For this spell you will be looking towards the goddess Venus and tapping into her power as giver of beauty. Remember, though, that while not everyone can have film-star looks, everyone can be beautiful, and you are aiming to maximise your physical attributes and inspire them with an attractive glow of inner beauty. Appreciating the beauty in you – both physical and mental – is what it is about.

Concentrate on your own image of Venus in your mind and direct your power towards personal beauty. Now take the red candle, dress it with love oil candle dressing and say:

I name this candle for my lips, that they be red, full and soft and speak only kind words.

Return the candle to the altar. Next take up the candle that is the colour of your skin, dress it with oil and say:

I name this candle for my complexion. May my skin be clean and clear and always free from blemish.

Place this candle beside the red one. Dress the candle that is the colour of your hair with love oil and say:

I name this candle for my hair. May it grow thick, strong and glossy and always be well kept and sweet smelling.

Add this candle to the altar. Now take up the candle that is the colour of your eyes, dress it with oil and say:

I name this candle for my eyes. May they always be bright, never to be dulled by life's sorrows and tears.

Place this candle on your altar and light all four candles from a single flame. Now repeat the following:

> *Blessed Venus, be my friend,*
> *Let my days of loneliness end.*
> *Grant me beauty, pure as the dove,*
> *For beauty wins the gift of love.*

Let the candles burn down and remember that true love will always be attracted by your inner beauty.

A spell for marriage

Purpose of ritual: To move things forward and set the date.

Items required: White candle, rose oil, confetti, bride and groom cake decoration, envelope.

Suggested lunar phase: Full moon.

Dress the white candle with rose oil and place it at the centre of your love altar. Now sprinkle a ring of confetti around the base of the candle, and place a bride and groom cake decoration before it. Visualise yourself on your wedding day. See yourself and your partner as being blissfully happy and speaking your vows to one another with sincerity. Hold this visualisation as you light the candle. Now concentrate on your focused intent and repeat this chant nine times:

> *Bride and groom and wedding band,*
> *I give, I take, I offer my hand.*
> *I ask for the gift of true love's fate,*
> *Now is the time to name the date.*

Allow the candle to burn down, then scoop up the confetti and place it in a sealed envelope. When the date has been set, throw the confetti to the winds and prepare for the happy occasion.

Aphrodite spell to bring love

Purpose of ritual: To bring romance into your life.

Items required: Red candle, love oil, tiny pink sea shell, sand, craft knife, sheet of paper.

Suggested lunar phase: New moon.

For this spell you will be calling on the powers of Aphrodite, Greek goddess of love. Aphrodite was born of the sea and so all aspects of sea-life are sacred to her.

To begin with, inscribe the word 'love' on the red candle. Then dress the candle with love oil candle dressing. Now, take a match or lighter and gently begin to heat the wax about half way down the candle. As the wax begins to soften, press in the sea shell, gently but firmly. Be careful not to break the shell. Next, lay the candle on the paper and sprinkle a little sand over it. The sand will stick to the oil. Concentrate hard on your magical goal of love and empower the candle to its purpose. Now light the wick and allow the candle to burn down.

To increase passion

Purpose of ritual: To assist passion in an established relationship.

Items required: Bright, vibrant red candle, ylang ylang oil, cinnamon, mixed spice.

Suggested lunar phase: Full moon.

This spell is simple but effective. Dress the candle with ylang ylang as this oil is well known for its aphrodisiac qualities. Then roll the candle in a little cinnamon and mixed spice – not too much. The idea is to spice up your love life – not burn yourself out! Place the candle somewhere in the bedroom and light it. While the candle burns, enjoy a romantic home-cooked meal. This spell normally works within six hours, so time it carefully.

To invoke love's blessing

Purpose of ritual: To invoke Aphrodite's blessing of love.

Items required: Pink candle for gentle love, or red candle for passion, craft knife, rose oil, large scallop shell, sheet of red paper or card, scissors, pen, fireproof bowl.

Suggested lunar phase: Waxing moon.

This spell also uses the powers of Aphrodite, but it is more direct and could cause manifestation to occur more quickly – so be prepared. Inscribe the word 'Aphrodite' down the length of the candle, and dress it with rose oil. Light the candle and drip hot wax into the 'cup' of the scallop shell, then set the candle into the pool of melted wax. This will hold the candle steady.

Next cut the red paper or card into a notepaper-sized love heart. On this love heart write the following:

Hail to Aphrodite! I call on your power to bestow love and I ask that you increase my own power and help me find my true love. Shower us with the blessings of love. By the power in me, so mote it be.

Sign and date the paper, fold it in half and then hold it above the candle to catch light. Drop the spell paper into the fireproof bowl and allow it to burn. Scatter the ashes around your doorstep and let the candle burn down. Your true love will soon be at your door.

If you prefer not to call upon any goddess then feel free to improvise with your own words of power.

Persephone's pomegranate to bring passion

Purpose of ritual: To bring passion, mystery and intrigue.

Items required: One red candle, one black candle, large mirror (a dressing table would be ideal), oils of your choice, craft knife, two pomegranates, knife, spoon.

Suggested lunar phase: Full moon or autumnal equinox (21 September).

This spell, designed to bring you a passionate encounter, with an air of mystery and magic to it, is lovely to perform and makes a nice decoration for an autumnal love altar. Pomegranates are used as the fruit associated with Persephone (queen of the underworld).

Dress each of the candles with an oil of your choice. On the black candle inscribe the word 'mystery' and on the red candle inscribe the word 'love'. Cut both pomegranates in half. Take two halves and scoop out a little of the fruit. Use these two halves as candle holders, using melted wax to hold the candles in place. Set these candles before the mirror, one at each side, and light them from the same match. Now sit gazing into the mirror and candle-light, and visualise your ideal partner. Spin webs of dreams around this encounter and begin to eat the remaining two pomegranate halves. Continue to focus on your required goal until you have eaten all the fruit. Allow the candles to burn down and then bury them in the earth. Put the pomegranate candle holders beneath a tree or hedge for the wildlife to enjoy. Look forward to your 'brief encounter' and make sure you always look your best – just in case.

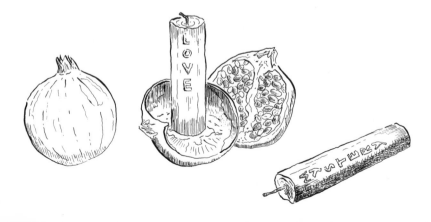

To dream of a lover

Purpose of ritual: To dream of a future love.

Items required: One blue candle, one red candle, lavender oil, dried lavender (some of it ground to a powder), love oil, dark-coloured thread, heatproof saucer or metal tray, small cloth bag.

Suggested lunar phase: Full moon.

This spell will help you to have prophetic dreams of your future love. It may be someone you already know, or it could be someone you have yet to meet.

Take the blue candle and dress it with lavender oil, then roll it in dried ground lavender. Dress the red candle with love oil and once again roll it in ground lavender. Now bind the two candles together with a dark-coloured thread. Place the candles on a heatproof saucer or metal tray and take them into the bedroom. Light them and repeat this chant three times:

Receive this spell, blessed be. My true love's face in dreams I see.

Allow the candles to burn for at least 15 minutes to fill your room with the dreamy fragrance of lavender. Then snuff out the candles and go to bed. Repeat this ritual each night until you are left with candle stubs of two to three centimetres (about one inch) tall. Place these in a little cloth bag, and add plenty of dried lavender. Sprinkle the bag with lavender oil and hang above the bed or place under the pillow. This should ensure dreams of your true love.

Fertility spell

Purpose of ritual: To conceive a child.

Items required: One red candle, one pink candle, one white candle, three acorns, pentacle, spell paper, white thread, heatproof surface, some representation of babyhood (for example a rattle or a soft toy: this should be brand new and will be your first present to your child).

Suggested lunar phase: Waxing moon.

This spell is best done at dawn when all life is stirring. The acorns (an age-old symbol of fertility) should be charged on your pentacle for three nights prior to the spell. You should also prepare a spell paper on which you have written your need for fertility and the safe birth of a healthy child. Once these have been charged, take them to your altar, along with the candles. Do not dress the candles, but simply bind them together with the white thread. The red candle should be positioned above the pink and white candles. Place the candles on a heatproof surface and light them. Put the three acorns around the candles to form a triangle. Now take the item that you have chosen to represent babyhood and place this in front of the candles. Lastly, really focus your power and concentrate on your need for a child to love and protect. As you do this, burn the spell paper. Allow the candles to burn out. Bury one of the acorns in the earth, and place the other two beneath the bed to work their fertility magic.

Cupid's arrow spell

Purpose of ritual: To become close again after an argument.

Items required: White candle, craft knife, large dressmaker's pin, small box.

Suggested lunar phase: Full moon.

This spell will help to ease the pain of a recent argument with a partner. Take the white candle and inscribe your partner's name on to it. Now take the pin and say:

I name you for Cupid's arrow – may your magic work as well.

Gently and firmly, press the pin through the candle, ensuring that it goes through your partner's name. Light the candle and repeat this spoken charm nine times:

Out frost, in fire,
Anger be replaced with desire,
Cupid's arrow pierce this heart,
My love and I will never part.

Allow the candle to burn out. The pin will fall as the candle melts. Place the pin in a box on your love altar. It is now Cupid's arrow and is safe for if it is needed again!

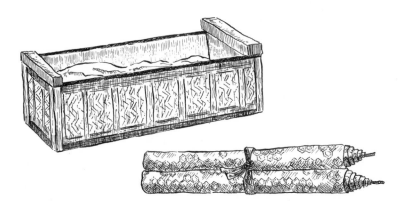

To heal a rift

Purpose of ritual: To heal a rift within a marriage.

Items required: Two red candles, your and your spouse's wedding rings, pentacle, love oil, lavender oil, rosemary, red ribbon, photograph of you and your spouse.

Suggested lunar phase: Waxing moon or full moon.

Use this spell to heal old hurts that are threatening your marriage. Or perform it after a major upheaval or disagreement between the two of you.

First prepare both of the wedding rings by leaving them on your pentacle for at least 24 hours to be charged with healing love. Dress both candles with love oil and lavender oil (a well-known healing oil) and then roll them both in rosemary (a herb of love). Thread both of your wedding rings on to the red ribbon. Now put the candles on your love altar, as far apart as your space will allow. Tie one end of the red ribbon to the candle on the left and the other end of the ribbon to the candle on the right, pulling the ribbon taut. Your wedding rings should now be suspended between the two candles. This acts as a bridge between the two of you, with the wedding rings, a symbol of eternal love, meeting in the middle. Place a photograph of the two of you sharing happier times beneath the ribbon bridge.

Now light the candles and focus on strengthening your marriage. Allow the candles to burn down almost to the ribbon. Snuff out the candles and remove the ribbon, tying the two ends together and leaving the rings in place. Put the ribbon and rings on your pentacle and leave them there for three days and nights. On the third night, allow the candles to burn down, replace the wedding rings on each other's fingers and renew your love in a physical, as well as emotional way.

Wax talisman of banishment

Purpose of ritual: To banish one who pesters you.

Items required: Black candle, greaseproof paper, thorn, craft knife, narrow black ribbon.

Suggested lunar phase: Waning moon or dark moon.

Sit at your candleburning altar (not the one dedicated to love) and light the black candle. Focus completely on the one who is harassing and pestering you. Feel your strength. Feel your magic. Be fully aware of your power. Now drip the wax on to greaseproof paper to form a pool of melted wax. Make a hole in the top using a thorn and say:

> *May this thorn pierce your balloon of interest.*

When the wax has hardened, inscribe your harasser's initials (or a question mark) into it and then strike them out by inscribing a cross through them. Hang the talisman on black ribbon and wear it around your neck, tucked under your clothes. You could also place these talismans over doorways to your home, in your car, in your desk at work and on your talisman tree.

To dispel negativity after an argument

Purpose of ritual: To renew harmony and peace.

Items required: White candle, a cleansing incense (sage or pine), craft knife, pine oil.

Suggested lunar phase: Full moon, or day following argument.

In the room where the argument took place, begin by opening windows and burning the incense. Now inscribe the candle with the words 'peace' and 'harmony', and dress it with pine oil. Hold the candle in your hands and concentrate on these powerful attributes. Place the candle in a prominent place within the room, for example in the fireplace, on the dresser, or in the centre of a table that is laid for a romantic 'all is forgiven' meal. Light the candle and let the magic do its work.

To sever the ties that bind

Purpose of ritual: To release yourself from lost love.

Items required: Two black candles, black thread, sharp scissors.

Suggested lunar phase: Waning moon.

Take the candles and name them, one for yourself, the other for your ex-partner. Bind the candles together with black thread, and say:

Thus we once were.

Then take the scissors and say:

I sever the ties that bound us together,
In mind, body, spirit and heart.
I sever the ties that bound us together,
For we must part.
I wish you well, I know the pain will heal,
But I sever the ties and break our seal.
So mote it be.

Cut the thread and light the candle bearing your name. Take the other candle and float it away on a living body of water such as a stream or an ocean. As you do this, release all regret and pain. Ask the waters for the gift of healing for all concerned.

Heartsease spell

Purpose of ritual: To heal an emotional wound.

Items required: One blue candle, one pink candle, a potted pansy, book or flower press, pink envelope, pen.

Suggested lunar phase: Waxing moon.

Take the two candles and stand them on either side of the pansy. Pluck a few of the pansy petals and hold them in your hands. Visualise them draining you of all emotional pain. Light the pink candle, naming it for self-love. Continue the visualisation, and feel free to shed a few tears as this will help you to release the pain. Now light the blue candle and name it for emotional healing. As the candles are burning, press the pansy petals in a book or flower press. Allow the candles to burn out. A month later, take the pressed pansy petals and seal them in a pink envelope. Write 'self-love is true love' on the envelope and put it somewhere safe

To heal old wounds

Purpose of ritual: To heal an emotional wound.

Items required: Blue candle, sharp object (optional), old blunt knife, soft cotton wool, piece of bandage.

Suggested lunar phase: Full moon.

Take the blue candle and with a sharp object or your fingernail, make a few scratches across it. Light the wick and say:

I light this candle for my wound of …

naming the hurt you feel. Now take the old blunt knife, and heat the blade in the flame of the candle. When the knife is hot, rub it along the scratches on the candle. Keep doing this until the wax is smooth and you have healed the candle of its wounds. Then leave the candle to burn freely until it is two to three centimetres (about one inch) tall. Wrap the stub in cotton wool, bind with a piece of bandage and then bury in the earth.

To enjoy independence

Purpose of ritual: To embrace 'singleness' and independence.

Items required: White or gold (for a man) or silver (for a woman) candle, photograph of yourself alone (or with a pet) and smiling happily, pad of paper, pen.

Suggested lunar phase: New moon.

Being single doesn't have to be a bad thing. In fact it can be a very good thing. It can be an opportunity to 'find' yourself, and to do all the things you felt that a relationship stifled. Work this spell as soon as you feel ready to embrace a single life and live it to the full.

First, clear everything off your candleburning altar. Place your photograph in the centre of the altar, put the candle behind the picture and light it. Write on the top line of your pad of paper:

I embrace my life as a single person.
Within the next twelve months I am going to …

Now write a long list of all the things you plan to do now that you are free to do them. This could be learning a new skill such as driving, swimming or self-defence. It could be redecorating your house entirely to your own taste, or saving for an expensive possession you've always wanted. Now you have time to yourself to write that book, take that holiday and catch up with old friends.

Read the list back to yourself and add new things such as going to the cinema or theatre on your own. Or booking a table for one at your favourite restaurant. You can bet your life unhappy couples will be envying you!

Pick one of the items from your list and do it within the next seven days. Then tick it off. Place the list under the candle and snuff out the flame. Every time you put a tick on your list, light the candle for a couple of minutes and embrace your freedom. See – life as a single person isn't so bad.

CHAPTER 9

Flames of prosperity

Prosperity is a state of mind. This is easy to say if you are rich and, perhaps, harder to accept if you are poor, but it is true nevertheless. Sympathetic magic demonstrates that what you focus on in life is exactly what you get. Therefore think wealth and you will be wealthy – but can it really be that simple?

Well, yes and no. The mechanics of money manifestation are quite easy to follow. The difficult part lies in re-programming yourself to think of money in an entirely different way. And this is where people new to money magic fail. Money is just another form of energy, so it can never die out and it can never truly be taken away. It can only change form. As a magical person you will be moving energy around all the time in all of your spells, and you must realise that money magic is no different – you are simply moving the energy that is known as money into your life.

As mentioned before, poverty and lack are man-made problems, and abundance is the natural way of the universe because the universe is unlimited. All you have to do is hold out your hand, state your need, focus – and manifestation will occur. It is as simple as that! Those who fail are those who cannot trust in their power to provide.

As with other aspects of magic, you must remain entirely focused on your magical goal and you must fully believe in your power and your ability to manifest money into your life. Another golden rule in money magic is that you must always add the words:

I cast this spell with harm to none

to every prosperity spell you perform. This is because money can sometimes come to you via an unpleasant or negative event, for example the death of a loved one, or compensation for an accident. So it is very important that you cast your spells in accordance with the 'harm none' rule. In this chapter you will find candle spells and rituals that will invite prosperity into your life. You will learn how to make your home a money magnet and will come to understand the positive effects of affirmations.

On the flip side of the prosperity coin is, of course, debt. Debt is a huge problem in today's society, but magic can assist with this too. Here you will find ideas to banish debt from your life, strengthen self-control over impulse buying and unnecessary spending, keep debt collectors and bailiffs from your door, and generally regain balance in your financial life. It is imperative that you work on both sides of the scale. For every debt-banishing ritual you do, you should also work a money-manifestation spell, say a prosperity affirmation, or sit for a while and magnetise abundance into your life. Always think of your personal finances as a pair of weighing scales. The idea is to put them into balance or lean them towards the prosperity side. This chapter will help you to do just that. And always remember to keep your thoughts positive when it comes to your personal finances.

You can adapt your candleburning altar to reflect aspects of prosperity and to assist further in the manifestation of money. This doesn't require a great change and is not in the same league as creating the true love shrine of the last chapter. Love has so many aspects to it that love magic comes with many rules, and can be a little complicated – thus warranting a space of its own. Prosperity magic is somewhat simpler.

The first step towards abundance is to be thankful for what you already have. For instance, you could write out a list of all the things in your life that you are grateful for, and place this on your altar. Then whenever you do a prosperity ritual you can literally 'count your blessings'.

Also, place something that is symbolic of wealth on your altar, such as a beautiful item of jewellery, a bag of coins, or gilded figures. A picture of Fortuna, Roman goddess of fortune would be appropriate, silver and gold candles, and an altar cloth of gold or silver tones would all add a sense of wealth and prosperity to your candleburning altar. You might also like to keep a loadstone, which is a natural magnet, on your altar and charge it with the powers of abundance and prosperity.

One thing I have found very useful in money manifestation is a money jar. In fact I have several. I keep my money jars on a table in the hallway, literally attracting more of the same to come through the front door. And it works. I strongly recommend that you collect two or three jars or bottles (pretty ones if you can find them), and begin collecting small denomination coins. I have four money jars altogether, each holding a different type of coin. This is a clever way of constantly keeping money in the house. It accumulates much faster than you might expect and you can use some of the money (never empty the jars completely) for emergencies, to go towards paying off a debt or to treat yourself.

Prosperity oil candle dressing

Purpose of ritual: To create an oil suitable for all prosperity spells.

Items required: Bowl, sunflower oil, pine oil, patchouli oil, dragon's blood oil (available from occult stores and by mail order), mint (optional), dark bottles, labels, pen.

Suggested lunar phase: Waxing to full moon.

You will probably want to make quite a lot of this prosperity oil, so make sure you have enough bottles to keep it in. It is a very powerful mixture and the following amounts will last you quite a while. Measure out one cup of sunflower oil – used because of its association with the sun and its golden yellow colour. These are powerful correspondences in prosperity magic.

Add to the sunflower oil five drops of pine oil, five drops of patchouli oil and three drops of dragon's blood oil. Once again use only pure essential oils. Stir this mixture with your finger and transfer it into dark bottles. If you like, you can add a sprig of mint to each bottle. Now label the bottles 'prosperity oil'. You can use this oil to dress all your prosperity candles, spell papers, and so on. You should also rub some of it on to your purse or wallet and dab a little on to any cheques you send out to ensure this money returns to you. If you work from home, are self-employed or are expecting any money by post, dab a little on to your letter box to ensure prompt payment.

Wax talisman of prosperity

Purpose of ritual: To bring prosperity into your life.

Items required: Green candle, greaseproof paper, patchouli oil, dried basil, craft knife, knitting needle or pencil, narrow green ribbon.

Suggested lunar phase: Waxing to full moon.

As with the talismans of love and friendship (see pages 74 and 75), drip hot wax on to greaseproof paper until you have a pool of melted wax. Now add a single drop of patchouli oil and a pinch of dried basil (a money-drawing herb). Whilst the wax is still malleable, place a hole in the top of the talisman using the knitting needle or pencil. Once the wax has hardened, inscribe either the amount of money you require, or a simple pound or dollar symbol. Thread the talisman with green ribbon and hang it on your talisman tree. You should also make one of these talismans and keep it in your wallet or purse.

Prosperity affirmation

Purpose of ritual: To affirm your right to abundance.

Items required: Silver, gold, green or white candle.

Suggested lunar phase: Waxing moon.

An affirmation is a positive statement that defines the need as if manifestation has already occurred. Words have power and affirmations hold magic. Sit before your altar and charge the candle with the powers of abundance. Now close your eyes and see yourself living free from the trouble of financial worry. Imagine yourself being able to pay bills easily, go out shopping, treat yourself and your loved ones and still have a healthy bank balance. Set the candle in the middle of the altar and say:

I name this candle abundance.
As it burns, so prosperity flows into my life.

Then begin to speak the following affirmation:

I have food to eat, I have a home,
I have the means of light and warmth,
I have lots of friends, I have family,
May my life be filled with prosperity.

Repeat this chant at least three times as the candle burns, and at any time when you feel anxious about money. Let the candle burn down. Remember that by acknowledging what you already have, you will attract more into your life. Try to perform this little candle ritual every week. Your wallet should soon begin to feel the benefit.

To magnetise abundance

Purpose of ritual: To bring abundance and prosperity into your life.

Items required: White candle, green pen, loadstone (a natural magnetic crystal available from occult stores or by mail order).

Suggested lunar phase: Waxing moon.

Sit before your altar. Make sure you are comfortable as you may be here for a while. Charge the candle with your magical goal. Take a green pen and write 'abundance' on one palm and 'prosperity' on the other. Don't worry about any money troubles you may have. Now place a loadstone before the candle and light the wick. Position your hands on either side of the candle, with your palms open and upwards. Close your eyes and visualise cash flowing into your waiting hands. Repeat this chant:

I magnetise prosperity and abundance.

Continue for as long as you are focused and comfortable. Then let the candle burn out and go about your day.

Green dragon of prosperity

Purpose of ritual: To invoke dragon power and bring prosperity.

Items required: Green candle, craft knife, prosperity oil, a representation of a green dragon (such as a figurine, a postcard or a book cover).

Suggested lunar phase: Full moon.

Take the green candle and inscribe the word 'dragon' on to it. Now dress it with prosperity oil. Place the representation of the green dragon before the candle and light the wick. Say the following chant five times:

> *The green dragon comes over the land,*
> *He takes away debt and puts cash in my hand.*
> *The green dragon comes over the sea,*
> *He brings prosperity and abundance to me.*
> *The green dragon comes out of the sky,*
> *He provides all I need for my family and I.*

Allow the candle to burn away and acknowledge the realm of the dragon in some way, such as by watching the film *Dragonheart*.

Salt spell

Purpose of ritual: To bring money to your purse.

Items required: Green candle, craft knife, prosperity oil, salt, sheet of newspaper or kitchen towel, purse or wallet, tissue (optional).

Suggested lunar phase: Waxing moon.

For many years salt was used as a form of money. In fact, the word 'salary' dates from those times. In this spell you will be calling upon the powers of salt to strengthen your sympathetic magic.

Take the green candle and inscribe it with the word 'prosperity', then dress it with prosperity oil. Now shake salt on to the newspaper or kitchen towel, and roll the candle so that it becomes evenly covered with the salt. Take a pinch of any salt that is left and put it in your purse or wallet – you can wrap it in tissue first if you like. Next, light the candle and concentrate on attracting the gifts of prosperity and abundance. Allow the candle to burn down naturally while you concentrate on the spell.

Rice spell

Purpose of ritual: To attract wealth and riches.

Items required: Green, silver, or gold candle, rice, mortar and pestle, prosperity oil, sheet of newspaper or kitchen towel.

Suggested lunar phase: Waxing moon.

This is a variation of the above spell using rice, which is also a symbol of money. To begin with you will need to grind up a few grains of rice using a mortar and pestle. Once you have ground the rice to a fine powder, dress the candle with prosperity oil and then roll it in the ground rice. Place the candle in the centre of the altar and light it. Watch the candle burn and as you do so, direct your power and focus entirely on your magical goal. Once you have released the power, go about your day and let the candle burn freely, keeping your eye on it to avoid accidents.

Acorn spell

Purpose of ritual: To draw money towards yourself.

Items required: Green candle, a fallen acorn, pentacle, craft knife, prosperity oil, piece of paper, pen, three coins, small bag, cash box.

Suggested lunar phase: Waxing moon.

As well as being a symbol of fertility, acorns are also used in prosperity spells and are well known among witches for their money-drawing qualities. For this spell, place the acorn on your pentacle and charge it with money-drawing powers. Now take the candle, inscribe a picture of an acorn on it and dress it with prosperity oil. Empower the candle with money-drawing powers and then set it in the middle of the altar and place the acorn before it. On a slip of paper, write the following words:

My home is blessed with abundance,
may money come to me from all directions.

Light the candle and focus on your goal. Later, when the candle has burnt down, place the acorn, the spell paper and three coins into a little bag. Keep this in a household cash box to draw money towards you and work its magic.

Pine cone spell

Purpose of ritual: To attract wealth.

Items required: Two green candles, two pine cones (fully opened), bowl of sand, pine oil.

Suggested lunar phase: Full moon.

This spell can be quite tricky, but it is very powerful and also makes a lovely winter altar decoration. Pluck away the top part of the pine cones, leaving you with two cup-like structures. Use these as candle holders by sitting them firmly in a bowl of sand. Dress two green candles with pine oil and repeat the required sum of money three times. Now set the candles in the pine cones and light them. Allow them to burn for three minutes, and as you do so, chant the sum of money you need. When the three minutes are up, snuff out the candles and say:

[The sum I require] is coming to me. This is my will, so mote it be.

Repeat this process daily until both candles are only two to three centimetres (about one inch) above the pine cones. Then remove the candle stubs and bury them in the earth. Put the pine cone holders in your spell box ready to use in the future.

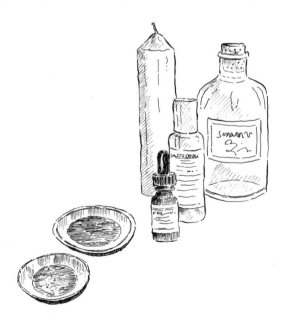

Mint and money spell

Purpose of ritual: To bring prosperity into your life.

Items required: Green candle, bowl, mint, cinnamon, sheet of newspaper, craft knife, patchouli oil, candle holder, three silver coins.

Suggested lunar phase: Waxing moon.

In the bowl, mix together equal amounts of mint and cinnamon, and spread out the sheet of newspaper in preparation. Take up your inscribing tool and carve the amount of money you need into the wax of the candle. Next, dress the candle with patchouli oil until it is completely covered.

Pour the mixed herbs on to the sheet of newspaper and gently roll the candle over them. The herbs will stick to the oil. Continue to roll until the candle is completely covered, and return the remaining herbs to the bowl. Now put the candle in a holder and place three silver coins around it to form a north-facing triangle. North is the direction of earth, and is associated with prosperity and abundance. Remember to keep your focus strong and clear. Light the candle and take up the bowl of herbs. Go around your home in a clockwise direction, scattering small pinches of the herbs in all corners, and on doorsteps and windowsills. If a few herbs remain, scatter them at your garden gate, or at the entrance to your property. Leave the spell candle burning to do its work. Afterwards, place the coins in a special place where you will not be tempted to spend them.

Prosperity candle wreath

Purpose of ritual: To attract wealth.

Items required: Large pillar candle of green or white, prosperity oil, bayberry oil, bayberry incense, florist's oasis ring, selection of fresh greenery such as holly, ivy, mistletoe, bayberries, acorns and pine cones, florist's wire, florist's card, pen.

Suggested lunar phase: Full moon.

Take the pillar candle and dress it in both prosperity oil and bayberry oil. Burn bayberry incense to enhance your ritual. Now take the florist's wreath and begin to decorate it with the greenery. Use florist's wire to attach the acorns and pine cones. Now splash the whole thing with prosperity oil. Attach a florist's card on which you have written the words:

> *I am a magnet to money, abundance, prosperity and wealth.*
> *Money flows to me.*

Sign and date the card. Place the wreath in a place where you can see it regularly so as to remind you of your goal. Put the pillar candle in the centre of the wreath and light it. When the candle has burnt down almost to the bottom and the greenery has faded, bury the whole thing in the garden, close to your front door. There it will continue to work its magic and will attract prosperity and wealth to your door.

Ivy spell for savings

Purpose of ritual: To keep your savings safe.

Items required: Green candle, craft knife, ivy, contents of wallet, cheque-book.

Suggested lunar phase: Full moon.

This spell is ideal if you have savings that you do not wish yourself or anyone else to touch. It works to guard your finances from frivolous spending. Take the green candle but do not dress it with oil. Inscribe it with the amount you have saved in figures. Now take a small tendril of ivy and bind it around the base of the candle, saying:

I bind my savings and make them grow.
Protect my interests, be it so!

Concentrate on your savings being completely safe from yourself and others, and focus on the amount continuing to increase. Now light the candle. When the flame reaches the ivy, snuff it out and remove the binding. Place this with your credit cards, cheque-book and so on, to prevent unnecessary spending. Re-light the candle and allow it to burn down.

Cinnamon and tea spell

Purpose of ritual: To bring money during a financial crisis.

Items required: White candle, prosperity oil or sunflower oil, tea bag, bowl, cinnamon, sheet of newspaper, green or white thread.

Suggested lunar phase: Any time, as this is an emergency spell.

If you ever find yourself in a state of serious financial stress, work this simple little spell. You will need only a white candle, which you should dress with either prosperity oil, or plain sunflower oil if that's all you have. Now take a tea bag and empty its contents into a bowl. Add a teaspoon of cinnamon and stir. Empty the contents of the bowl on to a sheet of newspaper and roll the candle through them. Concentrate on financial help coming to you, with harm to none. Light the candle and let the magic work. Fold up the corners of the newspaper with the remaining herbs on it and form a little bag, containing the spell powder. Tie the neck with a green or white thread. Place this near your front door, on your candleburning altar, or in a household cash box.

Spell for material possessions

Purpose of ritual: To manifest what you need.

Items required: White candle, picture of what you need (or pen and paper), patchouli oil, candle holder, envelope.

Suggested lunar phase: Waxing moon.

Find a picture to represent whatever it is you need, be it a new washing machine, television, cooker or a holiday. You could cut this out from a catalogue or if you cannot find a picture, simply write your need on a spell paper. Now dress the candle with patchouli oil and place the paper or picture beneath the candle holder. Light the candle, and as you do so, concentrate on magnetising your need into your life. Allow the candle to burn down. Take the picture or spell paper and seal it in an envelope. Once your need has manifested, burn the envelope without opening it. I have used this spell many times and it has always brought me exactly what I wanted.

Funny money spell

Purpose of ritual: To increase your wealth.

Items required: Green, gold or silver candle, child's pretend paper money (Monopoly money is ideal), bath or kitchen sink.

Suggested lunar phase: Waxing moon.

Take one of the highest denomination notes and wrap it around the base of the candle. Say this charm as you light the candle:

Take this money, blessed be, multiply my wealth by three.

Place the whole candle in the bath or kitchen sink, as the paper will catch fire. Continue the chant for as long as you remain focused. Let the candle burn, but keep a careful eye on it.

Manifesting money pot

Purpose of ritual: To bring a little extra financial help.

Items required: Pillar candle; medium-sized terracotta plant pot; glitter, markers, stickers, stamps or paint; prosperity, patchouli and bayberry oils.

Suggested lunar phase: Any time, as this is an emergency spell.

Decorate the terracotta pot with words and symbols that speak to you of wealth and prosperity. Dress the pillar candle with prosperity, patchouli and bayberry oils, and place it inside the pot. Put the whole thing on your altar. Now, whenever you have need of a little extra money, light the candle and concentrate on manifesting money for yourself. As soon as your focus begins to waver, snuff out the candle.

Prosperity scattering powder

Purpose of ritual: To attract prosperity to your home.

Items required: Tea-light candle, pentacle, mortar and pestle, pine needles, cinnamon, ground coffee, tea leaves, dried basil, dried mint, lantern.

Suggested lunar phase: Full moon.

On the night of the full moon, place a tea-light candle on your pentacle to charge it with the powers of prosperity. Using a mortar and pestle, grind together equal parts (about a teaspoon each) of pine needles, cinnamon, ground coffee, tea leaves, basil and mint. Continue grinding until you are left with a fine powder. Put a pinch of this powder on to the surface of the candle, and place it into a lantern. Light the candle and stand or hang the lantern by the front door. Now take the spell powder and scatter it along windowsills, doorsteps, letter boxes and around the entire perimeter of your property. As you do so, visualise prosperity and abundance flowing to you from all directions. Allow the candle to burn down. Bring the lantern inside the following morning.

Prosperity pumpkin

Purpose of ritual: To attract a particular sum of money.

Items required: Tea-light candle, pumpkin, knife.

Suggested lunar phase: Full moon or Hallowe'en.

This is a similar spell to the one for bringing love in the last chapter. Hollow out the pumpkin and carve into its body the sum of money you require. Now hold the tea-light between your palms and empower it with the energy to manifest this money. Light the candle and carefully place it in the pumpkin. Put the pumpkin on your candleburning altar and allow it to work its magic.

Oak king and holly king spell

Purpose of ritual: To invoke the aid of the 'green man'.

Items required: Green candle, oak leaf (midwinter solstice) or holly leaf (midsummer solstice).

Suggested lunar phase: Full moon, or solstice night.

The oak king reins from 21 December to 21 June and the holly king reins from 21 June to 21 December. This spell is best worked twice a year on the solstice nights: 21 June and 21 December.

In midwinter, the oak king slays the holly king and brings us the light half of the year. So at the midwinter solstice, light a green candle and place an oak leaf before it. As the candle burns, ask for the blessings of the oak king and concentrate on the gifts of food, wealth and abundance manifesting for you and your family throughout his reign.

In midsummer, the holly king is resurrected and slays the oak king, bringing us the dark half of the year. So at the midsummer solstice, repeat the same spell, placing a holly leaf before the candle instead. In working this spell twice a year, you will ensure that the 'green man' aids you in providing for yourself and your family all the year round.

Prosperity bath

Purpose of ritual: To bring an added boost to your finances.

Items required: Green, gold or silver candle or tea-light candle, salt, three silver coins.

Suggested lunar phase: Waxing to full moon.

Empower the candle or tea-light with the powers of abundance. Set it on the far side of the bath, or a shelf, and light it. Now run yourself a hot bath, and into it add a little salt and three silver coins. Soak in the bath for as long as you can, while visualising your abundance. Afterwards, carry the candle to your candle-burning altar and put the coins in your spell box for future prosperity baths.

Wax talisman of debt banishment

Purpose of ritual: To help banish debt.

Items required: Black candle, greaseproof paper, knitting needle or pencil, craft knife, narrow black ribbon.

Suggested lunar phase: Waning moon.

Light the black candle and drip wax on to the greaseproof paper as before (see page 74). Put a hole through the top of the talisman, using the knitting needle or pencil. Wait until the wax has hardened and then scratch on to the surface the amount of money you owe. Now strike it out with a cross. Turn the talisman over and on the back inscribe the words 'be gone'. Thread the black ribbon through the hole and hang the talisman on your talisman tree.

Debt protector

Purpose of ritual: To protect your space from creditors.

Items required: Black 'human form' candle, white candle.

Suggested lunar phase: Waning moon.

Use this spell in conjunction with Morrigan's cloak (see page 118). Sit before your altar and charge the black candle with the powers of guardianship of your property. Light the candle. Now send out your personal power and form it into a human shape – this is called a thought form. Simply imagine a shadowy figure standing before you. This thought form is yours to command as it is an extension of your own power. Use either the following words or others of your own devising:

I name you my protector. You are a guardian against debt. Your purpose is to keep all creditors and bailiffs away from my property. This is my will, so mote it be.

See the thought form fade away like mist and allow the candle to burn down. Once your debts are cleared, light a white candle and recall the energy of the thought form, by visualising it being drawn back into yourself. The thought form is no more.

Morrigan's cloak

Purpose of ritual: To keep away creditors.

Items required: Two black candles.

Suggested lunar phase: Waning moon.

Morrigan is the Celtic goddess of war, and an excellent goddess of protection and darkness, thus protecting and hiding you from creditors. This spell will help keep away debt collectors and bailiffs. Empower both candles with the powers of banishment. Sit before your altar and visualise yourself being free from debt. Now light the candles and carry them to the centre of the house. Stand with your arms raised, a candle in each hand. Perform the following invocation:

Hail to thee, Morrigan, I call upon your power. I ask that you help me to guard my home and myself from all creditors, and keep them away until I am in a position to pay. So mote it be.

Now bow your head and gently lower your arms as if you were pulling a dark cloak around yourself. As you do this visualise Morrigan's cloak enveloping your home and property, thus making it invisible to your enemies – the creditors. Blow out the candle flames and sit for a moment in total darkness, feeling your new sense of security. Keep the candles and perform the spell once a month until your debts are cleared.

Snake spell

Purpose of ritual: To prevent frivolous spending.

Items required: Black snake candle (available from most occult stores), purse or wallet, cheque-book.

Suggested lunar phase: Waning moon.

Charge the snake candle with the powers of self-control over your spending habits. Light the candle and collect together all your means of spending, such as your wallet or purse, and cheque-book. On each of these things, draw a snake with your finger, and envision the snake biting you every time you reach for them. Be strong in your focus and allow the candle to burn down. Take out only the money you really need, and leave all other forms of money at home or in the bank. If you feel your control is slipping, repeat the spell.

Black pepper ritual

Purpose of ritual: To keep debt from your door.

Items required: Black candle, almond or olive oil, sheet of newspaper, ground black pepper.

Suggested lunar phase: Dark moon.

Take the candle and dress it with a neutral oil such as almond or olive. Now roll the candle in black pepper. Take the black pepper shaker and the lighted candle and walk around the perimeters of your property in an anti-clockwise, or banishing, direction. Shake the pepper as you go. Finally, shake a line of pepper along the doorstep and leave the candle in the hallway, or near the front door to burn out.

When they owe you

Purpose of ritual: To bring in money that is owed to you.

Items required: Green candle, craft knife, pen and paper or letter from a company that owes you money.

Suggested lunar phase: Full moon.

Inscribe the amount owed to you on the candle. Now write the name of the person who owes you money on the paper, and place this (or the letter from a company) under the candle holder. Light the candle and say this charm three times:

The money owed me arrives soon;
This spell takes effect by the next full moon.

Let the candle burn out. Your money will be with you shortly.

CHAPTER 10

Flames of protection

In today's society there are times when we might feel less than safe. Crime rates always seem to be rising and I'm sure we all know at least one person (maybe ourselves) who has been a victim of crime.

Whenever you feel a little on edge or uneasy, then get out your candles and perform a protection ritual. Often, all that is needed is a simple cleansing to dispel negativity. Occasionally, however, something a little more substantial in the form of a protection spell may be required.

As with other types of magic, protection rituals should be performed on a regular basis, and they should be thought of as a prevention rather than a cure. In other words, don't wait until your house is burgled to perform a house protection ritual. If you regularly perform some sort of protection magic, you will be much more in control. This does not mean that bad things will never happen to you, but with the aid of protection magic, any negativity in your life will usually be fairly mild, and intense magic will straighten it out.

You will notice that all the spells in this chapter should be worked at the time of the full moon. This is because protective magic requires the most powerful lunar phase. In addition to using these spells, always carry yourself like a victor, a warlord – not a victim. Learn to talk a good fight – most of life's bullies are far too cowardly actually to call your bluff. But just in case they ever do, think about taking a self-defence or martial arts class. You will then be powerful on both the magical and mundane planes. You will be nobody's fool, nobody's victim, and will be in total control of your destiny.

Protection of self

Purpose of ritual: To protect yourself on all sides.

Items required: White candle.

Suggested lunar phase: Full moon.

Sit before your candleburning altar and empower the candle with the powers of protection. You should already have cast your magic circle and you are now going to cast an inner circle of personal protection. Place the candle in a holder and light it. Now slowly and very carefully, pass the candle in a wide circle around your head, transferring it from one hand to the other behind and above your head. Do this three times, visualising the candle flame leaving behind it a circle of protective white light that envelopes you. Now say:

This circle of protection moves with me. It goes where I go. It bends when I bend. It protects me on all sides, from all things seen and unseen. So mote it be.

Leave the candle to burn down and go about your day, knowing that your protective circle is with you. If you prefer, and providing your visualisation is clear, you can cast this spell with an unlit candle, and then light the candle afterwards.

Protection of property

Purpose of ritual: To protect your property from trespassers.

Items required: White tea-light candle, lantern (or hollowed-out turnip with some kind of handle), protective dried herb (such as basil or clove).

Suggested lunar phase: Full moon.

Charge or empower the tea-light with the powers of protection and sprinkle it with the protective herb. Now put the tea-light into the lantern and light it. Take up the lantern and carry it around your property boundary, walking in a clockwise direction. Visualise a circle of white light being left behind the lantern. Walk this circle three times and say on completion:

> *This circle of light, the circle of power,*
> *Protect this property from this hour.*

For the best results, repeat this ritual daily.

Protection of family

Purpose of ritual: To protect your loved ones.

Items required: White candles, craft knife, metal tray, white cotton, salt.

Suggested lunar phase: Waxing to full or any time in case of emergency.

Go to your candleburning altar, taking with you as many candles as you have loved ones, including one for yourself. With the inscribing tool, carve the names of your loved ones on to the candles, one family member per candle. Stand all the candles together on a metal tray and bind them with white cotton, thus representing the bond of the family unit. Sit for a while and focus on a shield of protective white light enveloping your family and keeping them from harm.

Next, take the salt and pour it in an unbroken line around the candles to form a circle. Light all the candles from the same taper and allow them to burn down.

Protection of a vehicle

Purpose of ritual: To protect a vehicle from theft or vandalism.

Items required: White candle, craft knife, a protection oil, a protective crystal (see page 51), incense cone, pentacle.

Suggested lunar phase: Full moon.

Charge the white candle and inscribe it with the registration number of the vehicle. Dress the candle with a protection oil. Choose a protective crystal and a small cone of your favourite incense. Place both the crystal and the incense on your pentacle to be charged with the powers of protection. Now light the candle and hold your hands over the flame – not too close!

Close your eyes and see your car being engulfed in white light. Know that your vehicle is protected from all thieves and vandals.

Allow the candle to burn itself out. Next, place the crystal in the car, perhaps in the glove compartment, or in a pretty little bag hung from the rear-view mirror. Burn the incense in the central ashtray of the car (not while you are driving).

Protection of a pet

Purpose of ritual: To protect your pet from all forms of harm.

Items required: White candle, lavender oil, photograph of your pet (or slip of paper bearing your pet's name), small box of cotton wool.

Suggested lunar phase: Full moon.

Dress the candle with lavender oil and place it on top of the photograph or slip of paper. Concentrate your power on your pet being protected from all harm and then light the candle. Allow the candle to burn until it is about two to three centimetres (about one inch) tall. Then snuff it out and place the stub carefully in the box of cotton wool. Seal the box with wax from the candle, and put it in a safe place. Your spell is done.

Protection of personal space

Purpose of ritual: To protect your personal space at work.

Items required: White candle, small jar of sea salt, amethyst crystal, pentacle, almond oil, lavender oil, spring water.

Suggested lunar phase: Full moon.

Charge the jar of sea salt and the crystal on your pentacle over the weekend. Take the white candle and dress it with almond oil. Then sprinkle a little sea salt over the candle. Place this in the centre of your candleburning altar and light the wick. Now, in your mind's eye, see yourself walking around the perimeter of your personal work space. This could be an entire office, a machine, a cubicle or just your own desk. Make sure you visualise with clarity and keep your focus strong. Allow the candle to burn down completely.

On Monday morning, go into work a few minutes early. Recall your visualisation and move around the exact same space, spraying a solution of lavender oil and spring water. This will cleanse the area. Next, place the jar of salt in a drawer of your desk for emergency cleansings, and display the amethyst crystal on your desk. This will absorb any new negativity coming your way. Recharge the crystal and salt every full moon.

Protection against fire

Purpose of ritual: To protect against accidental house fire.

Items required: White candle.

Suggested lunar phase: Full moon.

Simply light the candle and focus on the flame protecting you and yours from all harmful forms of fire. This spell is effective against lightning, electrocution and even sunburn.

Protection when out alone at night

Purpose of ritual: To protect you from harm and ensure safe passage home.

Items required: White candle, a picture or a figurine of a dragon, unicorn, knight or something else you would like as your guardian, craft knife.

Suggested lunar phase: Full moon.

Take the candle and inscribe the name of the guardian you have chosen. I will use a dragon as an example. Now either put the candle on top of the picture, or place the statue before the candle. Light the wick and begin to visualise your guardian as a thought form. Address the thought form in the following way as you concentrate your power on your magical goal:

Mighty Dragon, I bid thee welcome. I request that you guard and protect me whenever I have need of you. Protect me from all harmful things both seen and unseen. Whenever I have need of you, simply visualising you in my mind will call you to my aid.
So mote it be.

Allow the candle to burn down. Now whenever you are alone or feeling unsafe, just visualise a huge dragon walking by your side. Talk to him in your mind to reinforce the connection. Know that you are protected. I usually envision a red dragon on my left and a silver white unicorn on my right. I also have a green dragon and a dark knight patrolling my property and guarding my house. It is a simple technique that works very well and I highly recommend it.

House blessing protection ritual

Purpose of ritual: To protect your boundaries.

Items required: Four tea-lights, four garden lanterns or pumpkin, or turnip, lanterns, pentacle, box of sea salt.

Suggested lunar phase: Full moon.

This spell will protect the perimeters of your property, helping to keep intruders out. It will also add to the positive energies around your home. Charge all four tea-lights on your pentacle with the powers of protection against all things. Once they are fully empowered, take them outside with the lanterns, matches and a box of sea salt. Begin at the north, or twelve o'clock position, of your property. Light the candle, and place it in the lantern, saying:

Protected be!

Now scatter the salt from that point until you reach the east, or three o'clock point, of your property. Set down the lantern, light the candle and say:

Protected be!

Continue to scatter salt until you reach the six o'clock point and repeat the process. Do the same at the west, or nine o'clock position. Now continue to scatter salt until you are back at the northern point. If you have to go through the house at all to do this ritual, then simply scatter a pinch or two of salt along the walls and in corners. When you reach your starting point you should be standing within a protective circle of salt, with four lanterns lighting the compass points. Leave the candles to burn down.

Shielding spell

Purpose of ritual: To create an astral shield around yourself.

Items required: Four tea-lights, four candle holders.

Suggested lunar phase: Full moon.

This works in the same way as the previous spell. Sit comfortably on the floor, and taking the tea-lights in your hands, empower them with personal protection. Close your eyes and see yourself walking with complete confidence, knowing you are protected by your magic. Put the tea-lights in their holders and place them at the four compass points around you. Light the north candle and say:

Spirits of earth, guardians of the north, I ask for your protection.
May you shield me from harm.

Go to the east, light the candle and say:

Spirits of air, guardians of the east, I ask for your protection.
May you shield me from harm.

Now move to the south, light the candle and say:

Spirits of fire, guardians of the south, I ask for your protection.
May you shield me from harm.

Finally, go to the west, light the candle and say:

Spirits of water, guardians of the west, I ask for your protection.
May you shield me from harm.

Now slowly raise your arms, palms upwards, and imagine four columns of coloured light rising up from the four quarters: green from the north, yellow from the east, red from the south and blue from the west. These lights lock together to form an elemental shield around you. You must remain within the circle until the tea-lights burn out, so make sure you have a bottle of wine, nibbles, a good book, view of the television or can listen to music from where you are. It is a lovely magical way to spend an evening. Once the candles have burnt out, the shield is released from the elemental world and will guard and protect you wherever you go. Its power lasts about seven to eight days, so renew it once a week, or choose another protection spell instead.

Protection from theft

Purpose of ritual: To protect personal belongings.

Items required: White candle, craft knife, almond oil, dried basil, sheet of newspaper.

Suggested lunar phase: Full moon.

Take the candle and inscribe it with whatever it is you wish to protect, for example your car, jewellery or television. If you wish to protect everything with one ritual, inscribe 'All that is mine'. Now dress the candle with almond oil and roll it in dried basil, a very strong protection herb. Light the candle and speak this simple charm nine times:

All the things that belong to me,
From this moment shall protected be.

Allow the candle to burn out.

Gargoyle of protection

Purpose of ritual: To invoke a gargoyle thought form.

Items required: White candle or tea-light (depending on the form of your gargoyle), gargoyle figure (this could be in the form of a candle holder, or a statue from a garden centre) or picture of a gargoyle (bought or drawn yourself).

Suggested lunar phase: Full moon.

Gargoyles have been used since medieval times to protect churches and other important buildings. If you can get one, a figure of a gargoyle will be more effective than a picture in this ritual.

Charge your candle with protection. Concentrate on sending your power into the gargoyle, effectively breathing life into him. He is now a magical tool, so command him to protect your home and all within it. Place him in an upstairs window, facing outwards. When night falls, light the candle, making sure all curtains are pulled aside so the candle can burn freely. Repeat this on a nightly basis, especially during the dark, winter months.

Protection from storms

Purpose of ritual: To protect against storms.

Items required: White candle.

Suggested lunar phase: Perform whenever there is a storm.

This is a very simple spell, yet I have found that it seldom fails. When the storm comes and you can hear loud thunder and see flashes of lightning, go to your altar, light a white candle and ask the storm spirits to pass quickly over your property without causing harm or damage. Allow the candle to burn for as long as the storm continues. When the storm has passed, snuff out the candle and keep it for the next storm that comes along.

Protection from malice and spite

Purpose of ritual: To stop any spite directed your way.

Items required: White candle, vinegar, salt, mirror (with prop if needed).

Suggested lunar phase: Full moon.

This spell will redirect malice and spite back towards its senders. Take the white candle and hold it in your hands. Think of those who mean you harm and repeat nine times:

I am protected from your spite.

Now sprinkle the candle with a little vinegar – not too much or the candle won't burn. Then add a little salt to cleanse. Now light the candle and hold a mirror so that the candle-light is directed away from you. Use something to prop and hold the mirror in place (or use an adjustable shaving mirror) and leave the room. Do not look back, but shut the door firmly and say:

It is done. What you have sent out, returns to thee,
By the power of three times three. So mote it be.

Allow the candle to burn down.

Key of protection

Purpose of ritual: To protect your home from burglary.

Items required: White candle, spare key (that does not fit any lock in your house), pentacle, ribbon.

Suggested lunar phase: Full moon.

Heat one side of the candle until the wax softens. Now take the key and press it into the wax to make an imprint. Remove the key and place it on your pentacle to be charged with protection from burglars. Light the candle and repeat these words:

> *Those who come with wicked intent,*
> *To break my door and steal my rent,*
> *Will promptly turn their tail and flee,*
> *Due to the magic of my protection key.*
> *So mote it be.*

Allow the candle to burn down completely, take the key and thread it with ribbon, the colour of which should speak to you of protection. My key is hung on red ribbon, as I see this as spelling danger to any who oppose its magic. Now hang the key above the front door.

Mirror of protection

Purpose of ritual: To repel negativity from your home.

Items required: White candle, small mirror (for example a make-up mirror, or a candle sconce with a mirror behind it).

Suggested lunar phase: Full moon.

Charge both the candle and the mirror with the power to repel all negativity. Now take them both to the hallway, or to a position near the main entrance to your home, and place the mirror directly opposite the door. This will repel and reflect back any negativity that enters your home. Now light the candle and allow it to burn, as this will absorb any negativity currently residing in your home. Try to perform this spell as often as possible to keep your home free from negative vibrations.

Protection from gossip

Purpose of ritual: To put a stop to malicious gossip.

Items required: White candle, lemon juice, paper and pen, black thread, lemon, knitting needle (or skewer).

Suggested lunar phase: Full moon.

Dress the candle very lightly with lemon juice and light it. On the spell paper, write the name of the person, or persons, who are gossiping about you. If you do not know who is responsible, write: 'Those who speak against me'. Concentrate on the candle flame and visualise the gossips being brought to justice, and their evil words melting away. Now roll the spell paper tightly and bind it with a piece of black thread. Make a deep hole in the lemon using the knitting needle or skewer. Insert the rolled-up spell paper into the lemon and seal the hole with wax from the ritual candle. Leave the candle to burn and bury the lemon in the earth. This spell will put an end to the problem, and will make sure that the gossips are left with a very sour taste in their mouths!

Phone protection

Purpose of ritual: To protect your phone from bogus calls.

Items required: White candle, lavender oil, tiger's eye crystal, pentacle.

Suggested lunar phase: Full moon.

Dress the candle with lavender oil and place the crystal on your pentacle. Charge them both with protection from nuisance calls. Now carry them to the phone. Dab a little lavender oil on the receiver of the phone and place the candle and crystal beside it. Now light the candle and let it work its magic. Leave the tiger's eye beside the phone, and inform the correct authorities of the problem.

Mail protection

Purpose of ritual: To guard against nuisance letters.

Items required: White candle, lavender oil, tiger's eye crystal, grater, pouch (to match your décor), protective herbs and oils of your choice (see page 51), pot pourri.

Suggested lunar phase: Full moon.

This spell is similar to the one above. Once again, dress the candle with lavender oil and charge both the candle and the tiger's eye with protection from nuisance mail. Dab lavender oil on to both sides of the letter-box and then light the candle. Allow it to burn until it is two to three centimetres (about one inch) tall, then snuff it out. Now grate the candle stub and put the wax shavings into the pouch with the tiger's eye, the protective herbs and oils, and the pot pourri. Hang the pouch on the door close to the letter-box.

Protection from illness

Purpose of ritual: To protect against common ailments.

Items required: White candle, blue candle, craft knife, lavender oil, white thread.

Suggested lunar phase: Full moon.

Take both candles and inscribe them with the word 'health'. Dress them with lavender oil and charge them with the powers of good health. Bind the two candles together with the white thread. Light them and leave them to burn. This spell is particularly effective if done before the autumnal equinox (21 September) to ward off winter coughs and colds.

Protection for wild animals

Purpose of ritual: To protect wildlife from harm, cruelty and extinction.

Items required: Brown candle, craft knife, an oil of your choice, fresh earth.

Suggested lunar phase: Full moon.

Herne the hunter, also known as lord of the greenwood and the wildwood lord, is the guardian spirit of the forest. All wildlife is sacred to him and falls under his dominion. Lend your power to his, in his efforts to save our beautiful wildlife.

Take the brown candle and inscribe the word 'Herne' on to it. Dress the candle with the oil of your choice and sprinkle the fresh earth on to it. Now light the candle and hold your hands towards it. Concentrate on sending your power to all the wild animals that may need it. Focus on the following: saving the fox from the hunt, saving the stag from the bullet, saving badgers from the baiters, saving rabbit, hares, hedgehogs and so on from the roads, saving all animals from human folly and cruelty. Now in your mind's eye, see Herne the hunter, with a pair of magnificent stag antlers at his brow, and watch as he takes the power you have sent him and uses it to gather the wildlife into his protection. Know that you have helped the wildwood lord in his quest and allow the candle to burn down.

Protection from astral attack

Purpose of ritual: To strengthen the aura against astral attack.

Items required: Four tea-lights, four candle holders.

Suggested lunar phase: Full moon.

This ritual will protect you from a build-up of negative energy, which may be manifesting itself as nightmares, illness or just a really bad day. This is done by strengthening your aura.

Lie flat on the floor and place the candles in holders around you – two at your ankles and two at your shoulders – not too close. Light them and lie back down. Relax. The candles are there to absorb all the negativity and burn it away. Now when you feel nicely relaxed, begin to breathe deeply. As you breathe out, breathe through your mouth and imagine that you are blowing protective white light into your personal aura (the astral space that constantly surrounds you). Continue until you are in a happier state of mind – this means that your aura is now back to full strength and the candles have burnt off the negativity. Work this spell once a month to keep up your defences.

Protection on a journey

Purpose of ritual: To ensure safe arrival at your destination.

Items required: White candle, craft knife, tiger's eye crystal, pentacle, pen and paper.

Suggested lunar phase: Full moon.

Take the candle and inscribe the name of your destination on it. Charge the tiger's eye on your pentacle as you write your destination on a spell paper. Put this on your pentacle too and leave for at least 48 hours. On the night before your journey, light the candle and concentrate your power on a safe passage both to and from your destination. Take the spell paper and mark it with two arrows, pointing in opposite directions. Allow the candle to burn down. Carry the spell paper and crystal with you on your journey. When you return home, burn the spell paper and acknowledge your power.

Angelic protection

Purpose of ritual: To call your guardian angel.

Items required: White, gold or silver candle, craft knife, pictures and figures of angels or an angel pin or pendant.

Suggested lunar phase: Full moon.

For the best protection – call on the angels. Inscribe the candle with the word 'angel', light it and concentrate on the flame. Call your angel in the following way:

> *Guardian angel bring your light.*
> *Make my future days as bright,*
> *Bring with you an angelic shield,*
> *As your mighty sword you wield.*
> *Embrace me with protective wings,*
> *Guard me from all harmful things,*
> *I call you here, your power to lend,*
> *And welcome the love of an angel friend.*
> *So mote it be.*

Allow the candle to burn out. Enhance this ritual with the pictures and figures, or charge and wear an angel pin or pendant.

CHAPTER 11

Flames of power

In this chapter you will find a selection of spells that will assist you in a variety of situations that are likely to occur in everyday life from achieving ambitions to relaxing and having sweet dreams.

Goal-setting technique

Purpose of ritual: To set a goal in life.

Items required: Pen, paper (maybe special stationery or a postcard).

Suggested lunar phase: Blue moon.

Make a list of all your ambitions for the coming year, and then keep this paper somewhere safe, where you can see it every day, such as pinned to the fridge, under your pillow, in your purse or on your candleburning altar. A good idea is to write your goals on a piece of extra-special stationery or on a lovely postcard. In this way you turn your goals into something beautiful, and your ambitions will be a pleasure for you to look at, especially if the postcard depicts an aspect of your goal – a picture of a thatched cottage could represent your dream home, for example.

Scrying to see the past or future

Purpose of ritual: To see visions of past and future events.

Items required: White candle; bowl of water, mirror, magnifying glass (all optional).

Suggested lunar phase: Throughout the year.

The simplest form of fire scrying involves lighting a plain white candle. Dim all the other lights in the room and then settle comfortably in front of the candle flame. Gaze steadily at the blue part of the flame, relaxing your eyes and blinking whenever you need to. Do not stare as this will strain your eyes and will make scrying more difficult. Let your mind wander as it will and you will begin to see pictures in your mind. If you have never tried any form of divination before, then you will probably see visions of your past. Scenes from childhood, memorable holidays, events that occurred only last week, will flit before your mind's eye. Try to see if there is a message within these visions. Are you being told to learn from the past? Is the answer to a current problem or dilemma hidden away in your childhood?

If you cannot find a message, then don't worry. Simply enjoy the recollections your power is showing to you. If your visions of past events are painful, then it may be that you need to come to terms with this pain before you can look to the future.

For the best results, you should aim to practise fire scrying regularly, at least once a week. Divination is a skill that needs to be learnt. As such, you must practise if you wish to improve this skill and so expand your power. In time, scrying will come to you with ease and you will see inner visions and flashes of both the past and the future. These visions will in turn help you to make better decisions and will give you a magical 'edge' on life. As you become more experienced in fire scrying, interpretation will not only become less difficult, it will become more accurate. You will have developed your intuition to such a high degree that you will be completely confident in acting upon it.

Once you are happy with your performance using a single candle, you might like to add other tools to your scrying sessions. Bowls of water, mirrors and magnifying glasses can all be used to create a different focus. In these divinations, you should gaze at the reflection of the flame rather than the flame itself. A mirror shows a situation from a different angle, a magnifying glass magnifies a situation so that it can be seen more clearly, and a bowl of water reflects the hidden depths of a situation.

Eternal flame

Purpose of ritual: To bring relaxation and a connection with the spirit.

Items required: Candle, beautiful candle holder or lantern.

Suggested lunar phase: Throughout the year.

In ancient Rome, perpetual flames were tended by the Vestal virgins and this is a practice that many magical people emulate. Churches of all different religions, particularly Jewish and Catholic places of worship, keep candles burning on their altars as a way of connecting with their chosen divinity. This too is a form of candle magic.

If you spend a lot of time at home, you can incorporate the practice of an eternal flame into your rituals. Buy a beautiful candle holder or a decorative candle lantern specifically for this purpose. Light the candle at the same time every evening and let it burn for at least an hour (or for as long as you are in the room with it – never leave a candle unattended). This will become your candle time and, as a quiet end to a busy day, you will find that it offers an excellent opportunity for meditation and relaxation.

To stop a bad habit

Purpose of ritual: To stop a habit.

Items required: Black candle, almond oil, sheet of newspaper, black pepper, pen and paper, black tissue paper.

Suggested lunar phase: Waning moon.

Take the black candle and dress it with almond oil. Now roll it in black pepper, which has banishing properties. On a spell paper write down the habit you wish to vanquish. Now focus on being totally free of this habit, without any negative side effects. Light the candle and burn the spell paper. Snuff out the candle, wrap it in black tissue paper and bury it away from your property.

To begin a new project

Purpose of ritual: To enhance a new venture.

Items required: White candle, craft knife.

Suggested lunar phase: New moon.

Take the candle and inscribe your new venture on to it (for example a new job, new hobby, new home). Charge the candle with the power of success and strongly visualise yourself succeeding in your new project. Now light the candle and allow the magic to be released as it burns.

Household cleansing ritual

Purpose of ritual: To cleanse the home of negativity.

Items required: White candle, lemon juice, incense cone.

Suggested lunar phase: New moon – full moon.

Dress the candle with a little lemon juice, which is well known for its cleansing powers. Light a cone of your favourite incense and place it in a central position in the home, from where its scent will pervade the whole atmosphere. Now light the spell candle and put it in a holder that can be carried easily. Begin at the hearth or main fireplace, and walk around the room in a clockwise direction saying:

I cleanse this space with the powers of fire.

Visit every room in the house, including those you don't use often, carrying the candle and repeating this charm. Now place the candle on your altar to burn down. Finally, sprinkle a little lemon juice on windowsills and doorsteps. Your home is now magically cleansed and free from negativity.

Spell for psychic development

Purpose of ritual: To increase your psychic powers

Items required: Purple candle, craft knife.

Suggested lunar phase: Full moon.

When you work on psychic powers it is better to work on one thing at a time. For example, you may want to develop your powers of divination. Decide which power you would like to enhance first and inscribe it on to the candle. Now hold the candle in your hands and empower it with the powers of psychic ability. Next, light the candle and have it before you as you practise your power. Perform this little ritual every time you plan to use your psychic power.

To encourage sweet dreams

Purpose of ritual: To help call the dream of your choice.

Items required: Dark blue candle, lavender oil, pen and paper.

Suggested lunar phase: Full moon.

As evening falls, take the candle and dress it with lavender oil. Carry the candle to your bedroom. On a slip of paper write down the type of dream you want to have. Concentrate hard on experiencing that dream – this is known as dream incubation. Now light the candle and put the spell paper next to it. When the candle has almost burnt down, your room will be filled with the scent of lavender. Burn the spell paper and get ready for bed. Snuff out the candle, get into bed and wait for the dream to come.

Multi-purpose spell

Purpose of ritual: To fulfil any chosen need.

Items required: One candle (the colour should correspond to your need), craft knife, tailor's pins (the type with the coloured bobbles on the ends), an appropriate oil.

Suggested lunar phase: As appropriate to your need.

Place the candle before you in a suitable holder. Cup your hands around it, focusing your magical intent into its body. Carve a single word, rune or symbol into the wax to represent your need. Continue to focus on your intent. Now place the pins (a maximum of nine) in a row before you, and dress the candle with an appropriate oil. Next, take up each pin in turn, and with extra focus, pierce the wax and push the pin a quarter of the way in. Continue with the remaining pins, until they are all embedded in the candle. Place the candle on your altar and light it. Allow it to burn completely. As the candle burns, the pins will fall out one by one, releasing their focused energy. Collect the pins and bury them in the earth.

Thank you to Kris at the Welsh shop Bell, Book and Candle, who gave me this spell.

To welcome spring

Purpose of ritual: To attune with the new season.

Items required: Pale green candle (like new leaves), cloths and ribbons of pretty pastel colours, vases of spring flowers (such as tulips and daffodils), a spring-time oil (such as bluebell), appropriate music and poetry.

Suggested lunar phase: New moon.

Decorate your altar with the cloths, ribbons and vases of flowers. Take the candle and dress it with the oil. Now light the candle and concentrate on all that the season of spring entails: new lambs, flowers, buds on the trees, chicks and spring rains. Welcome the season by opening your heart to it. Play Vivaldi's *Four Seasons*, read poetry that echoes the themes of spring. Go for walks. Do all you can to attune with spring. Allow the candle to burn out.

To welcome summer

Purpose of ritual: To attune with the new season.

Items required: Yellow candle (like the sun), candle holders and ornaments to represent sunshine, yellow and gold ribbons, vases of roses, a summer oil (sunflower or rose), a representation of your summer holiday (optional).

Suggested lunar phase: Full moon.

Decorate your altar with the candle holders, ornaments, ribbons and roses. Dress the candle with oil and concentrate on all the joys that summer brings: flowers everywhere, singing birds, humming bees making honey, long summer nights, cool iced drinks. If you are planning a holiday this summer, place some representation of this on your altar. Light the candle and, as it burns, enjoy the summer evening.

To welcome autumn

Purpose of ritual: To attune with the new season.

Items required: Orange or bronze candle (like the falling leaves), brown altar cloth, bronze, orange and gold ribbons, vase of wheat and poppies, bowl of dried corn, an autumn oil (blackberry, apple or poppy), fallen leaves, pine cones, acorns.

Suggested lunar phase: Waning moon.

Decorate your altar with the brown altar cloth, ribbons, wheat, poppies and bowl of dried corn. Dress the candle with the autumnal oil and as you light the candle, focus on the season of the harvest, and the joy of food throughout the long, dark months ahead. Prepare the house for the colder weather. Make an autumnal pot pourri with the leaves, pine cones and acorns that you have collected. Drink in the beauty and colours of autumn.

To welcome winter

Purpose of ritual: To bring in winter with joy.

Items required: Red and green candles (for holly leaves and berries), red and green ribbons and cloths, fairy lights (optional), wreath of evergreen, vase of fallen twigs, silver paint and 'snow' sprays, picture of a snow scene and a stag, a winter oil (such as pine), green thread.

Suggested lunar phase: Dark moon.

Decorate the altar with the ribbons and cloths, the fairy lights, the wreath of evergreen and the snow scene picture. Spray the twigs with the silver paint and 'snow'. Take both the candles and dress them with the winter oil and then bind them together with the green thread. Light them and think of all that winter has to offer: cosy nights before the fire, hot chocolate, snow and frost, hot stews, midwinter parties, chestnuts, hot spicy punches, Christmas trees and carol singers. Acknowledge all you have received and learnt during the past year. Allow the candles to burn and welcome the season of winter into your heart.

To pass examinations

Purpose of ritual: To help when sitting exams.

Items required: Yellow candle, craft knife, sunflower oil, sheet of newspaper, dried basil.

Suggested lunar phase: Full moon.

Take the candle and inscribe into the wax the name of the examination you wish to pass. Dress the candle with the sunflower oil and then roll it in basil, a herb of immense power. Now focus your mind on your magical goal of passing the exam. Light the candle and allow it to burn and work its magic.

To increase personal power

Purpose of ritual: To increase your power and feeling of control.

Items required: Purple and white candles, craft knife, purple thread.

Suggested lunar phase: Waxing moon.

Inscribe the purple candle with the word 'power'. Inscribe the white candle with your name and place this at the centre of the candleburning altar. Now place the purple candle at the left side of the altar and light them both. Concentrate hard on your personal power and feel your inner strength growing.

Now move the purple candle a little closer to the white one, repeat the visualisation and snuff out the candles. Repeat this process every day until the candles are side by side. Then bind them together with purple thread, light them and allow them to burn down completely.

To change a run of bad luck

Purpose of ritual: To bring good luck and fortune.

Items required: Black cat candle.

Suggested lunar phase: Full moon.

Cup the candle in your hands and empower it with the powers of good luck. Take as long as you need for this. It is important that you keep your focus free from negativity – this means that you should not dwell on any of the bad luck you feel you've been experiencing. Once the cat candle is fully charged, light it and look forward to a positive change in fortune.

To gain employment

Purpose of ritual: To help with a job search.

Items required: Green candle, a prosperity oil, sheet of newspaper, money-drawing herbs, pen and paper.

Suggested lunar phase: Waxing moon.

Employment brings money, so dress the candle with an appropriate prosperity oil and roll it in money-drawing herbs of your choice (see page 50).

On a slip of paper, write down the job you want or the area of employment you wish to work in. Also write down the hours and wage required, and any other requirements. Now light the candle and visualise yourself happily performing the tasks of this job. Burn the spell paper in the candle flame and say:

It comes to me.

Snuff out the candle. When you have gained employment, burn the rest of the candle.

To lose weight

Purpose of ritual: To assist in a diet or exercise plan.

Items required: Black candle, craft knife, sharp knife.

Suggested lunar phase: Waning moon.

Begin by inscribing your target weight on to the black candle. Now take a sharp knife and pare away some of the wax from all sides, thus making the candle thinner. Visualise yourself turning away your favourite non-healthy foods and enjoying exercise. Also see yourself at your target weight and notice how good you look. Light the candle and let the magic work.

To pass a driving test

Purpose of ritual: To help when taking a driving test.

Items required: Yellow candle, a power oil, sheet of newspaper, power herbs, provisional driving licence.

Suggested lunar phase: Full moon.

Dress the candle in the chosen power oil and roll it in one or two power herbs (see page 51). Place it in a holder and put this on top of your provisional driving licence. Pour all your focus and power into the candle. Know that you will pass your driving test, that you will be reasonably confident and will keep any nerves under control. Next, visualise yourself driving your own car with complete confidence and safety. Now light the candle and allow it to burn down naturally.

Note that this spell will only work to enhance your confidence in your proven ability. It will not work if you are still a danger to yourself and other road users. If this is the case you should keep learning and try again later.

To create harmony at home

Purpose of ritual: To create a feel-good space.

Items required: Candle of any colour, except black, floral oil, sheet of newspaper, herbs or dried flower petals, incense, wind chimes.

Suggested lunar phase: New, waxing or full moon.

First clean the entire house and throw away any unwanted and unused items – this will make way for new things to enter your life. Dress the candle with a beautiful floral oil and roll it in herbs or dried flower petals of your choice.

Open all the windows, play harmonious and soothing music. Now light the candle and carry it to every room of your house. As you do so, envision rainbows and golden sunlight filling your home, making it a very magical place. Take the candle and place it on the hearth or fireplace to burn down. Do something quiet for the remainder of the day and avoid the television, as this invites scenes of violence and aggression into your home. To enhance this spell, go around the house with burning incense and wind chimes, making three journeys in all.

To lay old ghosts to rest

Purpose of ritual: To release the pain of unresolved issues.

Items required: Black or brown candle, craft knife, black tissue paper.

Suggested lunar phase: Waning moon.

Inscribe the candle with the issue you would like to lay to rest. Or inscribe the name of the person who has hurt you in the past. Now pour all your negative emotions regarding that issue or person into the candle and light it. Allow it to burn for a few minutes as you focus on releasing the pain. Then snuff the candle out and wrap it in black tissue paper. Bury it away from your property.

To know the truth

Purpose of ritual: To discover the truth.

Items required: White candle, craft knife.

Suggested lunar phase: Full moon.

Hold the candle and think about the situation as you see it and know it. Inscribe the candle with the word 'truth' and light it saying these words:

> *As I light this flame of gold,*
> *I command the truth be told.*
> *By the power of this spell,*
> *Those who know the truth, will tell.*
> *So be it.*

Allow the candle to burn out completely and prepare to hear the truth. This spell usually takes effect within 24 hours. Remember that you may not hear what you want to hear, but the truth will out.

To release a negative emotion

Purpose of ritual: To let go of a negative feeling.

Items required: Black candle, craft knife, cheese grater, piece of paper.

Suggested lunar phase: Waning moon.

Inscribe the candle with the negative emotion you have been feeling, such as anger or jealousy. Now focus all this emotion into the candle. Light it and allow it to burn until it is two to three centimetres (about one inch) in height. Now snuff out the candle and grate it up using a cheese grater. Make a paper boat and name it for the negative emotion you are releasing. Put the grated wax into the boat and float it away on a living body of water (the ruling element of emotions and healing) such as a stream or ocean. Walk away without looking back.

Goal-setting candles

Purpose of ritual: To assist in goal achievement.

Items required: Candle of an appropriate colour for your chosen goal (see pages 57–8), craft knife.

Suggested lunar phase: Blue moon or waxing moon.

This very simple spell will magically connect your goal to the universal energies, thus making manifestation much easier.

Inscribe and name your candle for your goal (remember that you can only have one goal per candle). Empower the candle with your magical intent and visualise strongly your goal target as if you have already achieved it. Now light the candle and leave it to burn. For large goals you may prefer to use the power of the full moon and perform the spell every 28 days until manifestation occurs.

CHAPTER 12

Advanced candle rituals

In this chapter you will find a few banishing and binding spells which are for use only when you have achieved a high level of competence. They should only be used in extreme cases and with the correct back-up action in the mundane world. Before using a binding or banishing spell you must be absolutely certain that it is the only way to go and you must also be sure of your motives.

A banishing spell that has been miscast can go tragically awry and can place a large blot on your karma copy book. A single binding spell can take many months of counter-active spell working to undo – and I speak from personal experience.

Warning: *These spells are not to be dabbled with – they are strictly for emergency use only.*

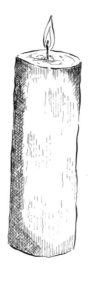

The Morrigan banishing

Purpose of ritual: To bind individuals from doing you harm and banish them from your presence.

Items required: Black candle, black fabric, black ribbon.

Suggested lunar phase: Dark moon, midnight.

First you should call on the powers of the Morrigan by saying:

I call upon the powers of the Morrigan, queen of witches, to assist me in my magical working this night. Hail to the warrior goddess! I bid you welcome and ask for your aid and protection.

Hold the black candle in both hands and empower it to its purpose by saying:

I charge this candle with the powers of the battle queen. May the wrath of the Morrigan bind [here state the name of your adversary] from doing me harm and banish [him/her] from my presence.

Now visualise yourself free of the person who means you harm. Envision this person staying right away from you and anyone connected with you. Know that this person can no longer cause you pain and that you are free of them. See how Morrigan stands between you and your foe, and know that your foe is aware of her presence and will not come near you. Now light the candle and say:

I light this candle in the name of the Morrigan. May she bind, banish and bring to justice those who would do me harm.

Snuff out the candle and say:

The flame has been banished to darkness – just as […] has been banished from my life.

Now wrap the candle in black fabric and tie it tightly with a black ribbon saying:

The binding is finished and […] is banished! I am the magic, the magic is me. As I will it, so shall it be!

Bury the candle and its bindings a couple of kilometres (about a mile) from your home or at the nearest crossroads. Be safe in your magical protection.

Morgana's karmic retribution spell

Purpose of ritual: To bring karma down on someone who has wronged you.

Items required: Black candle, craft knife.

Suggested lunar phase: Dark moon.

Take the black candle and inscribe it with the name of the one who has wronged you or done you harm. Charge the candle with karmic power. Light the wick and repeat this charm three times:

> *Punish the ones who cause us pain,*
> *Prevent them doing harm again*
> *Bring the rain and make it pour*
> *Bring them sorrows by the score.*
> *For every word they speak in spite*
> *Strike them down with all thy might*
> *For every action done in hate*
> *Bind them tight and seal their fate.*
> *Punish them one by one until*
> *Karma's cup has had its fill*
> *With witches' skill and Universal Power*
> *Make this then their darkest hour!*
> *So mote it be.*

Allow the candle to burn down.

A simple binding

Purpose of ritual: To bind one who means you harm.

Items required: Black candle, craft knife, black thread.

Suggested lunar phase: Dark moon.

Once again, inscribe the candle with the name of the person or people who mean to harm you. If you do not have a name, inscribe a question mark. Take a very long piece of black thread and begin to wrap it around the candle, slowly repeating the following chant:

> *Take them, bind them, round and round,*
> *Stop them, gag them, free from sound,*
> *I take the fire from the south*
> *And purge the evil from their mouth,*
> *I take the hatred from their heart,*
> *And there the seed of love doth start.*
> *Until they come in gentle guise*
> *Remove this person from my eyes.*
> *Bind them, wrap them, tie them tight,*
> *Remove this person from my sight!*

Continue until all the thread is wrapped around the candle. Now light the wick, place the candle in the bath and leave it to burn. This spell should take effect within 48 hours.

Afterword

Now it's your turn. Try any of the spells that appeal to you and feel free to adapt them to your own personal needs. I would love to hear from you, my magical reader, and know how this book has helped you. You may write to me via my publisher, but please enclose a stamped addressed envelope if you would like a reply.

Always remember that the magic is in you – in your heart, your head and your hands, not in the tools you use. This means that you can work magic anywhere, with anything. You have a very powerful tool at your disposal. Use it wisely. Turn your dreams into reality.

I hope that you have enjoyed reading this book as much as I have enjoyed writing it. Farewell my friend, until our next merry meeting.

Blessed be.

Morgana (Marie Bruce)

Index